Architectural Design Collaborators

3

Perlman/Stearns Inc.
80 Trowbridge Street, Cambridge/Massachusetts 02138

**Special thanks to the many people
whose support has been invaluable.**

Rita Perlman
Lori Perlman
Milton and Lanie Goldenberg
Larry and Sylvia Stearns
Kathy Furst
Nathan Furst

Mel Ingalls
Steven Trustman
Kevin Bottomley
Gardner McCormick

David Wasserman
Larry Schwartz
Bill Strong

Clifford Selbert Design

Lisa D'Ambrosio
DeFrancis Studio
Wendy Lurie
Theodore and Alice Thibodeau
Bill Harris
George Turnbull

Frank Costantino, ASAP
David Fraher, Arts Midwest
Elizabeth Goodrich, IDSA
Marion Greene, IALD
Lynn Learned, BCG
Jacquie Schiewe, IBD
Sarah Speare, SEGD
Richard Weisgrau, ASMP

Credits

Publisher/President	**Robert W. Perlman**
Vice-President, Marketing/Sales	**Arthur Furst**
Marketing/Sales Staff	**James Edwards** **Brian McCarron** **Christopher Burbul**
Systems Coordinator	**Ted Thibodeau, Jr.**
Marketing/Production Assistant	**M. Noel Page**
Production Manager	**Denise Kissel**
Graphic Design Consultant	**D.K. Design**
Copy/Layout Editor	**Melinda Baker**
Cover Photo	**James Edwards**
Printing/Color Separations	**Toppan Printing Co.** **(America)**
Distributed exclusively worldwide by	**Rockport Publishers, Inc.** P.O. Box 396 5 Smith Street Rockport/Massachusetts 01966 Telephone: (508) 546-9590 Fax: (508) 546-7141 Telex: 5106019284 ROCKORT PUB

Printed in Singapore

The A/DC staff is comprised of professionals in marketing, photography, illustration and graphic design. This balance of skills exemplifies the firm's commitment to the spirit of collaboration. In that spirit, A/DC encourages design professionals and industry organizations to contact the firm and share ideas on further enhancing communications among the design professions. For more information on participation in A/DC, call 617.497.1213.

ISBN# 0-9624219-4-4

TABLE OF CONTENTS

ASAP

■ American Society of Architectural Perspectivists

National Office c/o:

Boston Architectural Center
320 Newbury Street
Boston, MA 02115

617 536-3170

Philosophy and Purpose

The American Society of Architectural Perspectivists (ASAP) was founded in 1986 as a representative organization to foster communication among architectural perspectivists, to raise the standards of design drawing and illustration worldwide, and to acquaint a broader public with the importance of sustaining design as an adjunct to architectural design.

ASAP believes that by recognizing, celebrating, and disseminating the highest achievements in architectural drawing and painting, the quality of the work — and the working — will be heightened. With more sensitive, more accurate, and more professional architectural drawing, ASAP believes that architecture itself will be enhanced, resulting in benefit for all.

Membership

Membership is open to professional illustrators, architects, designers, students, and anyone engaged in the serious pursuit of drawing as a design and presentation tool in architecture. Overseas professional membership is available to international practitioners.

To encourage greater participatory opportunities for members and aspiring practitioners, active regional chapters are located in Chicago, Toronto, Seattle, Atlanta, San Francisco and Dallas. Advisory coordinators may be contacted in New York, Detroit, Philadelphia, St. Louis, San Jose and Calgary, Canada. International coordinators from several overseas countries serve as liaison to a growing overseas membership. Prospective members can request an international roster, with application, from the Society's headquarters.

Activities and Awards

The Society sponsors an annual competitive exhibition and convention, which brings together the best current work and practitioners of architectural drawing from the United States, Canada and around the world. Since their inception, ASAP's exhibits have been on show in major cities throughout the US as well as feature displays at AIA national conventions. The works are selected from submissions by a jury of respected professionals from the fields of architecture, illustration, and design education. The drawing judged to be the year's best of show may be accorded the highest award of the Society, the Hugh Ferriss Memorial Prize. ASAP, with funding from the Van Nostrand Reinhold Company, has established this award for excellence in the graphic representation of architecture. The Ferriss Prize is an award of a specially cast medallion, presented to the winner at the Society's convention.

Publications

ASAP publishes *Architecture in Perspective*, an annual catalogue featuring the selected work of each year's exhibition. Distributed by ASAP and VNR through bookstores, universities and mail order, the catalogue contains information on each artist and his/her respective drawing. Each of the five editions still available (1986 AIP III — 1991 AIP VI) serves as an invaluable reference source of services for the architectural and related professions. The catalogue is effective in broadening the exposure and increasing the geographic market base of many member illustrators.

Architecture in Perspective: A Five-Year Retrospective of Award-Winning Illustration, published by Van Nostrand Reinhold, is a hardcover book compilation of the exhibition catalogues and is available in most bookstores.

The Society provides a quarterly newsletter, *Convergence*, an attorney-designed standardized delineator's contract, and a national membership roster to its members. Transcripts of seminars on business practice and drawing issues are also available.

Special Programs

ASAP in conjunction with AIA, serves as a national clearing house and referral agency for architects and developers seeking the services of perspectivists. The Society sustains substantial world-wide communications with foreign affiliate organizations, i.e., the British Society of Architectural Illustrators and the Japan Architectural Renderers Association. Periodic contact is also maintained with the Australian, Chinese, Korean, German, Irish and other Asian and European rendering communities. Regular international exchange of drawings, slides and publications expands the scope of the illustrators' concerns and develops an understanding of foreign practitioners' work.

The Society annually sponsors seminars, workshops and lectures on a wide range of illustration techniques and business practices, both to its members and the architectural community. These are offered in conjunction with ASAP's and AIA's convention and at the various venues of our exhibit, *Architecture in Perspective*. ASAP likewise provides current information on legal issues and marketing practices.

■ Luis Blanc

Luis Blanc
30 St. Felix Street #2B
Brooklyn / New York
11217

718.797.1267

**Architectural Clients
Include**

Ahuja / Priya Architects
New York City

**Emilio Ambasz &
Associates**
New York City

John Burgee Architects
New York City

**Cooper / Roberson &
Partners**
New York City

**Gruzen Samton
Steinglass**
New York City

H.O.K.
New York City

**Philip Johnson
Architect**
New York City

Owens Engineering Inc.
Jackson, TN

Awards

Hugh Ferriss Memorial
Award 1991

■ William Gary Mellenbruch

Mellenbruch Studio Inc.
8118 NW Forest Drive
Kansas City / Missouri
64152

816.587.9565
800.345.DRAW Toll Free
816.587.2887 Fax

Providing quality architectural illustrations since 1969 for a diverse local, national, and international clientele.

Creative evolution has taken this artwork to a sophisticated level, using opaque gouache and transparent watercolor to create a blend that is tight architecturally but still has the loose qualities of watercolor. Original illustrations range in size from 20" x 30" to 30" x 40".

Full color brochure available upon request.

Selected Projects

1. Interior commercial building
Saudi Arabia
Architect:
Fayze Husseini
Manhattan, KS

2. Wadley Regional Medical Center
Texarkana, TX
Architect:
Richard D. Nelson
Omaha, NE

■ William Gary Mellenbruch

Mellenbruch Studio Inc.
8118 NW Forest Drive
Kansas City / Missouri
64152

816.587.9565
800.345.DRAW Toll Free
816.587.2887 Fax

Selected Projects

3. Embassy Suites Hotel
Sarasota, FL
Developer:
John Q. Hammons Industries
Architect:
Steve Minton
Springfield, MO

4. Galleria Complex
Tulsa, OK
Architect:
Architects Collective
Tulsa, OK

Architectural Clients Include

Nearing, Staats, Preloger & Jones
Shawnee Mission, KS

Hansen, Lind, Meyer
Iowa City, IA

Helmuth, Obata & Kassabaum
Kansas City, MO

Page Sutherland Page
Austin, TX

How Nelson & Associates
Omaha, NE

Sherlock Smith & Adams
Montgomery, AL

William Graves
Pensacola, FL

Vitols Associates
Boston

Environmental Design
Des Moines, IA

A.W. Nelson
Pine Bluff, AR

A.G. Spanos
Las Vegas, NV

J.C. Nichols Company
Kansas City, MO

Paragon Group
St. Louis, MO

■ Bruce Mayron

Bruce Mayron, BFA
Architectural Renderings
201 West 21st Street
Suite 15D
New York / New York
10011

212.633.1503

Mixing the best of perspectives drawn to scale with the trained eye of a fine artist.

Able to work within any budget. Fast turn around without sacrifice of quality.

Wide variety of styles available to accommodate any need. Very sensitive to illustrating the subtle qualities of each project.

Creates renderings - from plans or inspirational photographs - that will effectively sell the project.

Degree: Bachelor of Fine Arts Cum Laude in Interior Design, The Maryland Institute College of Art. Additional studies completed at the Art Students League of New York.

Clients Include

Reebok, Inc.

Helmsley Palace Hotel
(New York City)

Ponderosa Steakhouses

Metromedia

B.B. King

Barbie Doll International
(a division of Mattel Toys)

Hardy, Holzman, Pfeiffer

■ Michael McCann

Michael McCann
Associates, Ltd.
2 Gibson Avenue
Toronto / Ontario
Canada
M5R 1T5

416.964.7532
416.964.2060 Fax

An architectural rendering
company specializing in
watercolor perspectives
for an exclusive
worldwide clientele.

Founded in 1971.

Selected Projects

Euro-Disney
Paris
Architect:
**Skidmore, Owings &
Merrill**
New York City

Tokyo Forum Competition
Tokyo
Architect:
**James Sterling
Michael Wilford &
Associates**
London

Metropolitan Life Building
North Project
New York City
Architect:
**Kohn Pedersen Fox
Conway**
New York City

Jeddah Airport
Competition
Jeddah, Saudi Arabia
Architect:
**Skidmore, Owings &
Merrill**
Chicago

Disney Studios
Anaheim, CA
Architect:
**Cooper/Robertson &
Partners**
New York City

Portcullis Competition
London
Architect:
**Zeidler / Roberts
Partnership**
Toronto
London

■ Lee Dunnette

Lee Dunnette
21 Stuyvesant Oval
Suite 2E
New York / New York
10009

212.260.4240

Techniques

Ink rendering with
transparent color

Ink line drawing with
transparent airbrush color

Full-color opaque acrylic

Color acrylic
photomontage

Black Prismacolor pencil

**Architectural Clients
Include**

**Pei Cobb Freed &
Partners**
New York City

**Kohn Pederson Fox
Associates**
New York City

Hardy Holzman Pfieffer
New York City

Fox & Fowle Architects
New York City

**Hellmuth Obata
Kassabaum**
New York City

**Rafael Vinoly &
Associates**
New York City

**Cooper Robertson &
Partners**
New York City

Beyer Blinder Belle
New York City

**Costas Kondylis
Architects**
New York City

**Ehrenkrantz Eckstut &
Whitelaw**
New York City

■ Edward Dumont

Edward Dumont
1461 Pueblo Drive
Pittsburgh / Pennsylvania
15228

412.343.2544

Techniques

Felt tip and line
conceptuals for all areas
of design

Pen and ink

Watercolor washes
and glazes

Airbrush

Pastel

Prismacolor pencils

Matting and framing
for presentation

Architectural Clients Include

Bechtel National Inc.
New Martinsville, WV

Oxford Development , Inc.
Pittsburgh, PA

Williams / Trebilcock / Whitehead
Pittsburgh, PA

Bonita Bay Properties, Inc.
Bonita Springs, FL

L. Robert Kimball Associates
Edensburg, PA

Tasso Katselas Associates
Pittsburgh, PA

The Design Alliance
Pittsburgh, PA

IKM Incorporated
Pittsburgh, PA

GWSM Landscape Architects
Pittsburgh, PA

■ PRELIM, Inc.

PRELIM, Inc.
Robert Cook, President
8330 Medow Road #210
Dallas / Texas
75231

214.692.7226
800.541.0492 Toll Free
214.692.7286 Fax

Techniques

Edge to edge tempera

Vignettes

Special effects
(night scenes)

Pen and ink

Pen, ink, and watercolor

Photo montage

Computer-generated
perspectives

Selected Projects

1. JC Penny Corporate
Headquarters
Plano, TX
Architect:
HKS Architects
Dallas

2. Renaissance Center
Bridgeport, CT
Architect:
**Architects
Environmental
Collaborative**
New Haven, CT

3. JC Penny Corporate
Headquarters
Plano, TX
Architect:
HKS Architects
Dallas

2

3

Offering a selection of
the most beautiful and
innovative approaches in
the field of architectural
presentation. Known for
flexibility and architectural
precision, with a growing
national and worldwide
reputation for excellence.
Color brochure available.

■ Blackman Architectural Illustrators

Blackman Architectural
Illustrators, Inc.
150 SW 12th Avenue
Suite 310
Pompano Beach / Florida
33069

305.781.5302
305.781.5303 Fax

Techniques

Broadline Pencil

Pen & Ink

Felt-tip / Marker

Watercolor

Airbrush

A quarter of a century of accomplishments creating dramatic and appealing residential, commercial, and industrial architectural renderings. Proven success in both interior and exterior work, as well as hand and computer-generated designs.

A nation-wide reputation for exceptional quality and fast service within the client's budget and time constraints.

Projects successfully completed for architects, engineers, developers, interior designers, and industrial designers.

Fax and modem equipment allow for quick approvals and world-wide access.

Services

Presentations

Displays

■ Art Associates, Inc.

Art Associates, Inc.
4635 West Alexis Road
Toledo / Ohio
43623-1005

419.537.1303
419.474.9113 Fax

Services

Illustrations in any style

Advertising design and art

In-house photography and printing

Graphic arts, films, stats, veloxes, typesetting, and lithography

Computer animation, video imaging, and scanning, from wire frames to fully rendered images

Architectural, engineering, topographic, and product prototype models.

Desk reference with 185 color plates available on request.

1

3

4

2

Providing architects, engineers, developers, and advertising agencies worldwide with over 20,000 commissions since 1966.

■ Art Associates, Inc.

Art Associates, Inc.
4635 West Alexis Road
Toledo / Ohio
43623-1005

419.537.1303
419.474.9113 Fax

5

6

Selected Projects

1. Gran Central Center
Miami
Architect:
**Smallwood, Reynolds,
Stewart & Stewart**
Atlanta

2. Universal Studios
Theme Park
Orlando, FL
Client:
Universal Studios
Orlando, FL

3. Nationwide Insurance
World Headquarters
Columbus, OH
Architect:
BOHM NBBJ
Columbus, OH

4. Clemson University
Stadium
Client:
Graphics Plus
Greenville, SC

5. Church Interior
(photo retouch - area
between pews and light
fixtures is all painted in)
Architect:
Weibel Rudzewski
Erie, PA

6. Chase Retreat
Belize
Client:
Mars Advertising
Detroit MI

■ Tainer Associates, Ltd.

Tainer Associates, Ltd.
213 West Institute Place
Suite 301
Chicago / Illinois
60610

312.951.1656
312.951.8773 Fax

Architectural Clients Include

Skidmore, Owings & Merrill
Chicago

Lohan Associates
Chicago

Perkins & Will
Chicago

VOA Associates
Chicago

ISD, Inc.
Chicago

Powell / Kleinschmidt
Chicago

Pappageorge / Haymes Ltd.
Chicago

The Landahl Group
Chicago

Hague Richards Associates
Chicago

Swanke Hayden Connell Architects
Chicago

HOK
St. Louis

Camburas & Theodore, Inc.
Chicago

Horn & Associates
Chicago

Clients Include

RREFF Funds

Stein & Company

L.J. Sheridan & Company

JMB Realty

The John Buck Company

Tishman Speyer Properties

The Hoffman Group

Tanguay Burke & Stratton

Diversified Capital Group, Inc.

Pulte Home Corporation

United Development Company, Inc.

Balcor Development Company

The Prime Group

Limpro, Inc.

Rubloff, Inc.

Draper & Kramer, Inc.

Multi-disciplined design studio offering a full range of ink, marker, air brush, and mixed media illustrations.

Language Fluency: Italian, French, and Spanish

James Edwards, Illustration

James Edwards
Sherman Street Studios
7 Sherman Street
Boston / Massachusetts
02129

61/.522.2656
617.241.8344

Specializing in fine architectural watercolors for renovation and historical projects, incorporating lifelike human characters as they relate to specified environments.

Realistic treatment of the planned landscape and foliage in a traditional style and technique complements the technical accuracy of the architectural details.

Also experienced in illustrations for publication in marketing, advertising, and editorial materials.

Selected Project

Clocktower Place
Nashua, NH

Illustrations conveying the beauty, historic quality, and commercial potential of Nashua's newly renovated mill buildings.

Commissioned by the developer for use in a full color brochure and other sales materials.

Framed originals also showcased in the developer's on-site offices as sales tools for client viewing during the renovation and construction phases.

■ Richard Rochon

Rochon Associates, Inc.
13530 Michigan Avenue
Suite 205
Dearborn / Michigan
48126

313.584.9580
313.584.4071 Fax

Advisory Council:
American Society of
Architectural Perspectivists

Member: New York
Society of Renderers

Author: *Color in
Architectural Illustration*
(Van Nostrand Reinhold
1989)

Honorary Member:
Michigan Society of
Architects

1

■ Richard Rochon

Rochon Associates, Inc.
13530 Michigan Avenue
Suite 205
Dearborn / Michigan
48126

313.584.9580
313.584.4071 Fax

2

Architectural Clients
Include

1. **Skidmore, Owings & Merrill**
New York City

2. **Rossetti Associates**
Detroit

Arquitectonica
Coral Gables, FL
Chicago

Cambridge Seven Associates
Cambridge, MA

Ellerbe Becket
Washington, DC

Hellmuth Obata Kassabaum
New York City
Washington, DC

James Stewart Polshek
New York City

Skidmore, Owings & Merrill
Chicago

Smith, Hinchman & Grylls
Detroit

Minoru Yamasaki & Associates
Troy, MI

■ James C. Smith

The Studio of
James C. Smith
700 South Clinton Street
Chicago / Illinois
60607

312.987.0132
312.987.0099 Fax

Selected Project

The Rookery Building
Chicago
Developer:
**Baldwin Development
Company**
Chicago

Creating a serene sense
of design and pattern
while illustrating
architectural treatments,
this painting depicts the
restoration of the oriel
stairway and light court
of the Burnham & Root's
Rookery Building. It is one
of seven images that
detailed the restoration
concepts. The view was
constructed with
traditional methods and
shows the stained glass
with ornamental iron
patterns, various metal
components of the stair,
and the outer wall
assembly.

Clients Include

DeStefano / Goettsch

Murphy / Jahn

Perkins & Will

Skidmore, Owings &
Merrill
(Chicago &
Washington DC)

Trammell Crow Company

DePaul University

City of Chicago

Art Institute of Chicago

Techniques

Line & color illustrations

Airbrush paintings

Photographic retouching

Trompe l'oeil mural
painting

■ Lori Brown

Lori Brown
Consultants Ltd.
1639 West 2nd Avenue
Vancouver / British
Columbia
Canada
V6J 1H3

604.685.0401 Office
604.224.4035 Home
604.685.2795 Fax

Architectural illustration in mixed media ranging from loose concept sketches to final presentation drawings.

Selected Projects

1. Residential Project
Vancouver, BC
Architect:
Hancock Nicolson Tamaki
Vancouver, BC

2. Capilano College Library
N. Vancouver, BC
Architect:
Henriquez & Partners
Vancouver, BC

Expo '92
Seville, Spain
Concept Design & Illustration

Expo '86
Vancouver, BC
Color Program & Illustration

"Pearls of Kuwait"
Competition
Kuwait City, Kuwait
Architect:
Arthur Erickson Associates
Vancouver, BC

Member: American
Association of
Architectural
Perspectivists

■ Dan Harmon

Dan Harmon & Associates
2839 Paces Ferry Road
Suite 370
Atlanta / Georgia
30339

404.436.0854
404.333.8970 Fax

Awards

The American Society of
Architectural Perspectivists
1988, 1990

American Institute of
Architects (Atlanta
Chapter)
Service to the Profession
1980, 1989

Architectural Clients Include

John Portman & Associates
Atlanta

Thompson, Ventulett & Stainback
Atlanta

Cousins Properties, Inc.
Atlanta

Gerald Hines Interests
Atlanta

Carter & Associates
Atlanta

Interstate Hotels Corporation
Pittsburgh, PA

Marriott Corporation
Lakeland, FL

HOK
New York City

Odell Associates
Charlotte, NC

■ David A. Anderson

David A. Anderson
Architectural Illustration
PO Box 7055
1316 Chestnut Street
San Carlos / California
94070-4715

415.592.1868

Specializing in exterior
and interior acrylic
renderings for architects,
engineers, and developers.
Other presentation media
include pencil, pen and
ink, and pen and ink with
watercolor.

Member: American
Society of Architectural
Perspectivists

**Architectural Clients
Include**

**Design & Engineering
Systems, Inc.**
Redwood City, CA

**Leo A. Daly &
Associates**
San Francisco

Ehrlich • Rominger
San Francisco
Los Altos, CA

**Gensler & Associates
Architects**
San Francisco

GHI Architects
San Francisco

**Hornberger Worstell &
Associates**
San Francisco

**Kaplan • McLaughlin •
Diaz**
San Francisco

**McLellan &
Copenhagen, Inc.**
Cupertino, CA

**Bent Severin &
Associates**
San Francisco

**Orlando Diaz-Azcuy
Designs**
San Francisco

Selected Project

600 California Street
San Francisco
Architect:
**Kohn Pederson Fox
Associates**
New York City

Frank Costantino

F.M. Costantino, Inc.
13b Pauline Street
Winthrop / Massachusetts
02152

617.846.4766
617.846.4766 Fax

Delineation in the tradition of fine architectural drawing, providing the discerning client with distinctive illustrations of architecture.

Co-founder: American Society of Architectural Perspectivists

Fellow: Society of Architectural Illustrators (Great Britain)

Honorary Member: Japan Architectural Renderers Association

Please refer to A/DC 1 and 2 for further examples of work.

Selected Project

New Tanglewood Concert Hall (summer home of the Boston Symphony Orchestra)
Lenox, MA
Architect:
William Rawn & Associates
Boston

■ Frank Costantino

F.M. Costantino, Inc.
13b Pauline Street
Winthrop / Massachusetts
02152

617.846.4766
617.846.4766 Fax

Publications

*Architecture in
Perspective: A Five-Year
Retrospective of Award-
Winning Illustration*
(Van Nostrand Reinhold
1991)

Architectural Rendering
(Quarto Publishing Ltd.
1991)

*Architectural Delineation:
A Photographic Approach
to Presentation*
(McGraw Hill 1991)

Selected Project

Maxwell School
Syracuse University
Syracuse, NY
Architect:
**Bohlin, Cywinski,
Jackson**
Wilkes-Barre, PA

■ Gregory Cloud

Gregory Cloud Associates
2116 Arlington Avenue
Suite 236
Los Angeles / California
90018

213.484.9479
213.734.0515 Fax

**Architectural Clients
Include**

RTKL Associates
Los Angeles

Altoon & Porter
Los Angeles

Jerde Partnership, Ltd.
Los Angeles

**Walt Disney
Imagineering**
Los Angeles

AC Martin
Los Angeles

SDI
Los Angeles

**DeBretteville &
Polyzoides**
Los Angeles

**Steven Ehrlich
Associates**
Venice, CA

**Richard Magee &
Associates**
Los Angeles

**Johannes Van Tilburg
& Partners**
Los Angeles

Other Clients Include

Ahmanson Development

Maguire Thomas Partners

MCA Universal

Treptow Development

Caldwell Banker, REIBS

Dames & Moore

Robert Englekirk

JMB Realty

Chandler Group

The Ratkovich Company

Providing architects and
developers with
personalized service and
high quality illustrations
using traditional and
digital techniques.

Services include
presentation graphics, 3D
computer animation, and
photo services.

■ Thomas Demko

Thomas Demko
326 Maple Avenue
Pittsburgh / Pennsylvania
15218

412.242.3721

Selected Project

Carrie Furnaces
Pittsburgh, PA
study sketches
Architect:
**Landmarks Design
Associates**
Pittsburgh, PA

Offering a traveling
rendering service for quick
in-office sketches or
conceptual studies.

Works executed in pen
and ink line, watercolor,
marker, or acrylic.

■ Tamotsu Yamamoto

Yamamoto Architectural
Illustration
15 Sleeper Street
Boston / Massachusetts
02210

617.542.1021
617.451.0271 Fax

Services include watercolor, gouache, pen and ink, airbrush, other drawing media, and computer-generated perspectives.

Able to work with architect or developer in early stages of design conceptualization, creating quick sketches in any medium through final presentation drawings.

Instructor in architectural perspectives and illustration since 1979 at institutions including the Massachusetts College of Art and the Boston Architectural Center.

Member/Officer: American Society of Architectural Perspectivists

Member: Japan Architectural Renderers Association

1

Architectural Clients Include

The Architects Collaborative
Cambridge, MA

Architectural Resources Cambridge, Inc.
Cambridge, MA

Carlson Associates, Inc.
Cochituate, MA

Elkus Manfredi Architects, Ltd.
Boston

LEA Group, Inc.
Boston

Todd Lee Clark Rozas Associates, Inc.
Boston

Nikken Sekkei International, Inc.
New York City

Tufts University
Medford, MA

Daniel F. Tully Associates, Inc.
Melrose, MA

2

3

Selected Projects

1. Tufts University
Dormitory
Medford, MA
using watercolor as a
final presentation medium
Architect:
Architectural Resources Cambridge, Inc.
Cambridge, MA

2, 3.Examples of 24-hour service, using a technique that combines both watercolor and tempera.

■ Barbara Worth Ratner

Barbara Worth Ratner
828 Charles Allen Drive NE
Atlanta / Georgia
30308

404.876.3943
404.874.1264 Fax

Selected Projects

1. Fire Station #3
at Phipps Plaza
Atlanta
Architect:
**Roberts & Collins
Architects**
Atlanta

2. Broughton Street
Savannah, GA
Architect:
**Cooper Carry &
Associates**
Atlanta

1

2

**Architectural Clients
Include**

**Roberts & Collins
Architects**
Atlanta

**Cooper Carry &
Associates**
Atlanta

The Rouse Company
Columbia, MD

**Trammell Crow
Company**
Charlotte, NC

**Thompson, Ventulett,
Stainback & Associates**
Atlanta

**Space Design
International**
Cincinnati

Turner Associates
Atlanta

Arvida/JMB Partners
Boca Raton, FL

**SAE/Carlson, Carlson
Associates**
Atlanta

**Metropolitan Atlanta
Rapid Transit Authority**
Atlanta

Exhibitions

Architecture in Perspective
American Society of
Architectural Perspectivists
Los Angeles 1988
Chicago 1989
Boston 1990
New York City 1991

JARA Annual Exhibit
Tokyo 1991

■ William Hook

W. G. Hook
Architectural Illustrations
1501 Western Avenue
Suite 500A
Seattle / Washington
98101

206.622.3849

Publications

Architecture in Watercolor
Thomas W. Schaller
(Van Nostrand Reinhold
1990)

The Wright Space
Grant Hildebrand
(University of Washington
Press 1991)

Architectural Rendering
Gerald Green
(Quarto Publishing Ltd.,
London, 1991)

Streetcar Suburb
Casey Rosenberg
(Fanlight Press 1989)

Architecture in Perspective
Volumes II, III, V, & VI
(American Society
of Architectural
Perspectivists, 1987,
1988, 1990, & 1991)

*JARA 10th Anniversary
Exhibition*
(Japan Architectural
Renderers Association,
Tokyo, 1990)

**Architectural Clients
Include**

The NBBJ Group
San Francisco
Seattle

Wright Runstad & Co.
Seattle

INTEGRUS Architecture
Seattle
Spokane, WA

**Loshkey Marquardt
Nesholm**
Seattle

Zimmer Gunsul Frasca
Seattle

**Bassetti Norton Metler
Rekevics Architects**
Seattle

Olson Sundberg
Seattle

Buffalo Design
Seattle

University of California
San Diego
Irvine
Davis

Port of Seattle
Seattle

Registered architect with
extensive design
experience providing
design input and finished
illustrations with
transparent watercolor,
ink wash, pen and pencil.

■ Charlie Manus

Architectural
Presentation Arts
43 Union Avenue #1
Memphis / Tennessee
38103

901.525.4335
901.527.1143 Fax

Clients Include

ADG

Federal Express

Holiday Corporation

Plough Inc.

RCA Cylix

Vantage Companies

Trammell Crow

Weston Companies

Belz Enterprises

Richards Medical

Promus

JMGR

D. E. Miller & Associates

Hood-Rich

Forcum-Lannom, Inc.

Johnson Properties

Pyramid Companies

Selected Projects

1. City of Memphis Trolley Project
Memphis, TN
Architect:
Hnedak, Bobo Group
Memphis, TN

2. Hampton Inn
Boston
Architect:
Looney, Ricks, Kiss
Memphis, TN

3. Purchasing Facility
Sarasota County School Board
Sarasota, FL
Architect:
George Palermo & Associates
Sarasota, FL

1

2

3

Twenty-four years of providing high-quality renderings. Techniques include pencil, pen and ink, colored acetate, and air brush for site plans, elevations, vignettes, and full color renderings.

■ Richard Sneary

Sneary Architectural
Illustration
323 West Eighth Street
Kansas City / Missouri
64105

816.421.7771
800.886.7117

Publications

Architectural Record

Progressive Architecture

*Architectural Rendering
Techniques*
Mike Lin
(Van Nostrand, 1985)

*Architectural Drawing:
Options for Design*
Paul Lasseau
(Design Press, 1991)

1

Member: American
Institute of Architects;
American Society of
Architectural Perspectivists

■ Sam Ringman

Ringman Design &
Illustration
2700 Fairmount
Suite 100
Dallas / Texas
75201

214.871.9001

IR **45**

Architectural Clients Include

Hellmuth, Obata & Kassabaum
Dallas
London

Trammell Crow Company
Dallas
Los Angeles

Harwood K. Smith & Partners
Dallas

Corgan Associates Architects
Dallas

Omniplan
Dallas

Hermanovski Lauck Design
Dallas

Healthcare Environment Design
Dallas

Interprise / Southwest
Dallas

Herman Miller
Dallas

RTKL Associates
Dallas

Exhibitions

Annual Awards Exhibitions
American Society
of Architectural
Perspectivists
Chicago 1989
Boston 1990
New York City 1991

Registered architect
producing architectural
and interior renderings in
a variety of media,
including pen and ink,
pencil, colored pencil,
marker, and water color.

■ Rael D. Slutsky

Rael D. Slutsky &
Associates, Inc.
8 South Michigan Avenue
Suite 310
Chicago / Illinois
60603

312.580.1995
312.580.1980 Fax

A creative and
professional source for
the finest architectural
renderings. Staff of
architect-artists has
serviced an international
clientele for more than 14
years.

Drawing techniques range
from quick freehand
design sketches to formal,
detailed pen and ink
renderings. The process
yields both black and
white and color originals
of each image. Portfolio
furnished upon request.

Advisory Council
Chairman and Executive
Board Member: American
Society of Architectural
Perspectivists.

Member: American
Institute of Architects

Exhibitions

American Society of
Architectural
Perspectivists Annual
Awards Exhibition
1987, 1988, 1989, 1991

Japanese Architectural
Renderers Association
Annual Exhibition
Tokyo 1989, 1990

■ Rael D. Slutsky

Rael D. Slutsky &
Associates, Inc.
8 South Michigan Avenue
Suite 310
Chicago / Illinois
60603

312.580.1995
312.580.1980 Fax

**Architectural Clients
Include**

**Skidmore Owings &
Merrill**
(nationwide)

**Cesar Pelli &
Associates**
New Haven, CT

**Hellmuth, Obata &
Kassabaum**
St. Louis
New York City

**Kevin Roche John
Dinkeloo & Associates**
Hamden, CT

Murphy / Jahn
Chicago

Perkins & Will
Chicago

Holabird & Root
Chicago

Odell & Associates, Inc.
Charlotte, NC

Altoon & Porter
Los Angeles

**Pei Cobb Freed &
Partners**
New York City

Cooper Cary
Atlanta

RTKL
Dallas

Kunwon International
Seoul, Korea

Il Sin Architects
Seoul, Korea

Florence S. Nahikian

Florence S. Nahikian
286 Hackett Hill Road
Hooksett /
New Hampshire
03106

603.641.6418
603.645.6661 Fax

Practicing architectural communication since 1976 for an international clientele of architectural, interior design, landscaping, and development firms in the US, France, and the Middle East.

Expression techniques range from fluid conceptual sketches to formal , crisp renderings and complete presentations in a variety of media, such as pen and ink, graphite, color pencil, pastel, color marker, gouache, and watercolor.

Clients Include

A Wogenski (France)

Berthet-Godet (France)

P. Y. Taralon (France)

Schemes (Saudi Arabia)

Carur Inc.(Lebanon)

Seven Up (Nigeria)

Batimark Inc. (Canada)

Newstress International

Norwood Realty

Hoyle, Tanner & Associates

Howard Johnson

Epoch Corporation

NYNEX

Sunoco

Honda

Stein Consultants

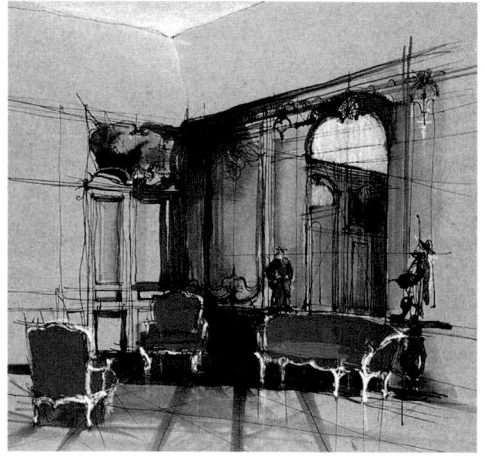

Member: American Society of Architectural Perspectivists

Degree: Master of Interior Architecture

■ Eric Schleef

Eric Schleef Illustration
7740 Dean Road
Indianapolis / Indiana
46240

317.595.0016
317.595.0016 Fax

Specializing in versatile line and mixed-media color illustration. Quick sketches, pencil, and watercolor techniques are also available. Able to work from conceptual sketches and working drawings, at the studio or on location with the design team.

Member: American Society of Architectural Perspectivists

Architectural Clients Include

Browning Day Mullins Dierdorf
Indianapolis

Group Eleven Architecture & Planning
Indianapolis

Howard Needles Tammen & Bergendoff
Indianapolis

Kasler & Associates
Cincinnati

The Odle McGuire & Shook Corporation
Indianapolis

Schmidt Associates Architects
Indianapolis

Swanke Hayden Connell Architects
Chicago

Tomblinson Harburn Associates
Flint, MI

Other Clients Include

Eli Lilly & Company

Kiwanis Magazine

Earlham College

Shuel Advertising

The National Art Museum of Sport

■ Richard C. Baehr

Richard C. Baehr, AIA
Architectural Rendering
305 Northern Boulevard
Great Neck / New York
11021

516.466.0470
516.466.1670 Fax

Selected Projects

1. The Court at One
International Place
Boston
Architect:
John Burgee Architects
New York City

2. Retail Arcade
The Bond Building
Sydney, Australia
Architect:
Kohn Pederson Fox
New York City

3. St. Charles Cemetery
Mausoleum
Long Island, NY
Architect:
**Angelo Francis Corva
& Associates**
Uniondale, NY

4. 270 Madison Avenue
Renovation
New York City
Architect:
**Max Gordon &
Associates**

1

2

Specializing in full-color
tempera renderings. Other
media include pencil on
mylar, pen and ink, and
photo montage.

Member: American
Institute of Architects;
American Society of
Architectural Perspectivists

■ Richard C. Baehr

Richard C. Baehr, AIA
Architectural Rendering
305 Northern Boulevard
Great Neck / New York
11021

516.466.0470
516.466.1670 Fax

Free
illus
with
toni
fand
renc

Mer
Arch
Can
Aso
Iord
Arch

Pres
Soci
Pers

3

4

Architectural Clients Include

Ammann & Whitney
New York City

Edward Larrabee Barnes
New York City

John Burgee Architects
New York City

Castro Blanco Piscioneri & Associates
New York City

Angelo Francis Corva & Associates
Uniondale, NY

Davis, Brody Associates
New York City

Costas Kondylis Architects
New York City

Mojo Stumer Architects
Roslyn Heights, NY

Cesar Pelli & Associates
New Haven, CT

Der Scutt Architect
New York City

Other Clients Include

Bellemead Development Corporation

Brookhaven National Laboratory

Gerald D. Hines Interests

The Trump Organization

Richard Zirinsky Associates

Barry N. Nathan

Barry R. Nathan
2666 East Bayshore Road
Palo Alto / California
94303

415.424.0980
415.856.3266 Fax

Architectural exterior and interior renderings in a variety of media and techniques, from loose pencil sketches to finished airbrush. 3D CAD capability.

Registered Architect

Member: American Association of Architectural Perspectivists

Selected Project

Proposed Hotel Casino
Queensland, Australia
Architect:
Robert Sprague
San Francisco

■ Barbara Morello

Morello Design Studios, Inc.
7 Jackes Avenue
Suite 1105
Toronto / Ontario
Canada
M4T 1E3

416.963.4315

Tacoma / Washington
206.572.6106

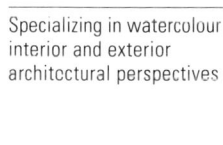

Specializing in watercolour
interior and exterior
architectural perspectives

**Architectural Clients
Include**

Carlos Ott
Toronto

Norr
Toronto

Housden Barnard
Los Angeles

Ziedler Roberts
Toronto

Barton Gillet
Baltimore, MD

Architekten RKW
Dusseldorf, Germany

WZMH
Toronto

Bregman Hammon
Toronto

HNTB
Alexandria, VA

■ Marty Coulter Studio

Marty Coulter Studio
10129 Conway Road
St. Louis / Missouri
63124

314.432.2721
314.432.2721 Cellular & Fax

Selected Projects

"Drachen Fire"
Roller Coaster at Busch
Gardens
Williamsburg, VA
Architect:
PGAV
St. Louis

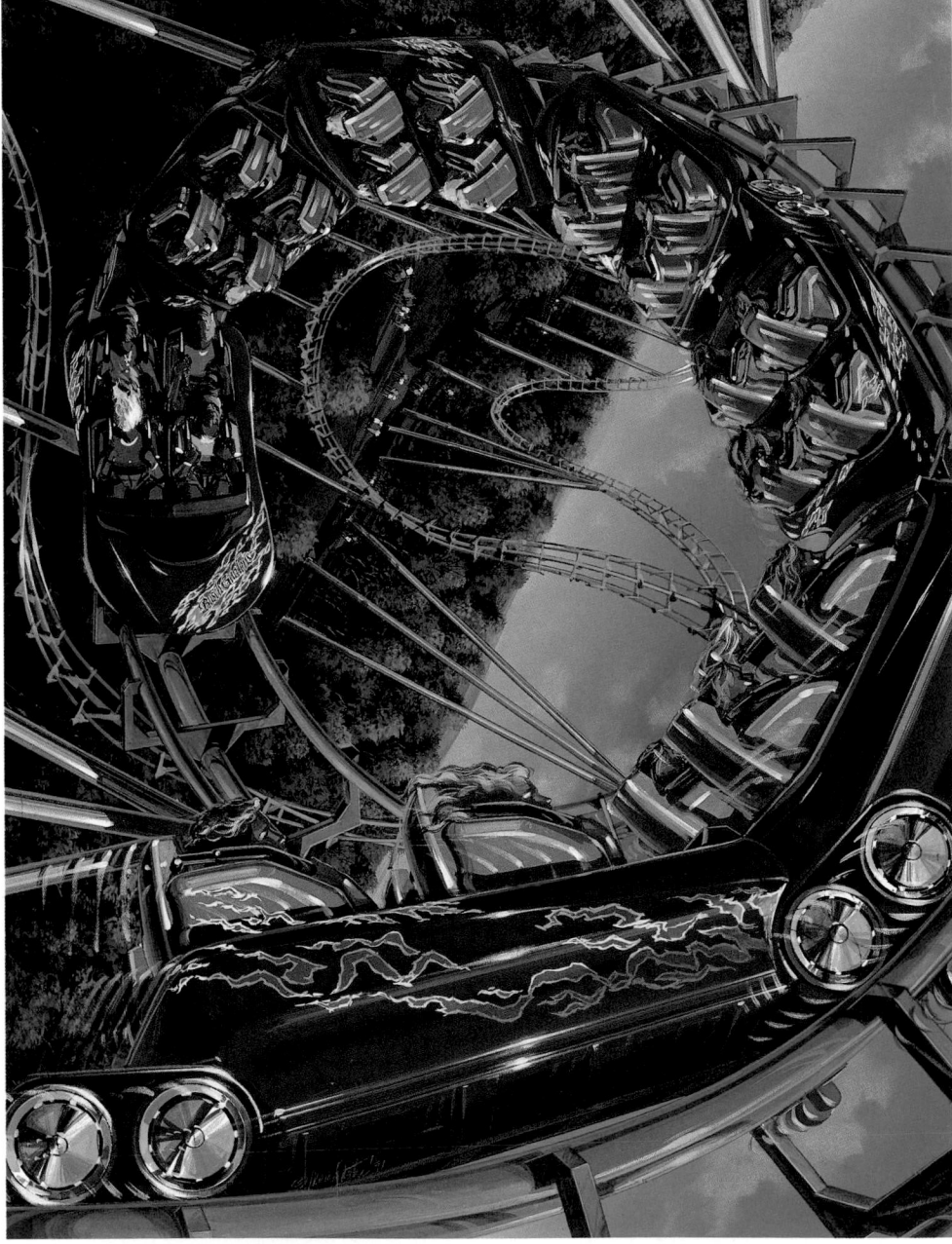

Clients Include

Peckham, Guyton Albers &
Viets

Hellmuth, Obata &
Kassabaum

Sverdrup Interiors Division

Michael Fox, Inc.

Pearce Corporation

Busch Entertainment
Corporation

Ralston Purina Company

Anheuser-Busch
Companies, Inc.

The Forsythe Group, Inc.

Missouri Botanical Garden

Maritz Communications
Company

Robinson, Yesawich &
Pepperdine, Inc.
(Orlando)

Illustrating architectural
and sometimes not so
architectural subjects for
many St. Louis companies
since 1968

© Busch
Entertainment
Corporation
1991

■ W. Kirk Doggett

Architectural Illustration
PO Box 1305
Suite 199
Brunswick / Maine
04011

207.729.4509

Renderings suited for use in design, presentation and marketing. Techniques include watercolor, graphite, and colored pencil. Computer generated pre-views are utilized to allow for client preferences and to assure satisfaction.

Former instructor of architectural rendering techniques at the Boston Architectural Center and Mount Ida College's Chamberlayne School of Design.

Member: American Society of Architectural Perspectivists

1

2

Architectural Clients Include

1. **Ward-Rovner Public Relations**
Boston

2. **Robert Durham / Architects**
Abilene, TX

Architectural Resources Cambridge
Cambridge, MA

Brim & Associates, Inc.
Danvers, MA

The Druker Company
Boston

The Flatley Company
Braintree, MA

The Hospitality Group
Northampton, MA

JSA Inc.
Portsmouth, NH

Wellesley Design Consultants
Wellesley, MA

Robert M. Wood Architects
Boston

Exhibitions

The Process of Architectural Perspective Rendering
Dana Gallery, Wellesley, MA
1991

ASAP Boston Members Show
World Trade Center, Boston
1990

David Joyner
Fred Davis
PO Box 11173
Knoxville / Tennessee
37939-1173

615.584.8334
615.584.8334 Fax

Providing a full range of quality architectural illustration.

Member: American Society of Architectural Perspectivists; Tennessee Watercolor Society

Professional Affiliate: American Institute of Architects (East Tennessee Chapter)

Architectural Clients Include

Barber & McMurry, Inc.
Knoxville

Lockwood Greene, Inc.
Oak Ridge, TN

McCarty Holsaple McCarty
Knoxville

Upland Design Group, Inc.
Crossville, TN

Tennessee Valley Authority
Knoxville

Whittle Communications
Knoxville

Martin Marietta Energy Systems
Oak Ridge, TN

Brewer, Ingram, Fuller
Knoxville

Lewis Moore Group
Knoxville

Design Specialties

Environmental Graphic Design

Lighting Designers

Specialized Services

Society of Environmental Graphic Designers Information

EGD

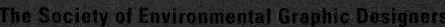 **The Society of Environmental Graphic Designers**

National Office:

47 3rd Street #201
Cambridge, MA 02141
617.577.8225

Attention
Sarah Speare
Executive Director

Philosophy and Purpose

The Society of Environmental Graphic Designers (SEGD) is an international, non-profit, professional design organization devoted to promoting public awareness and professional development of the field of environmental graphic design. The society, founded in 1973, is a committed group of over 700 environmental graphic designers, industrial designers, architects, landscape architects, interior designers, researchers, educators, and manufacturers involved in three-dimensional visual communication design. Members' work ranges from exhibit design to large-scale sign systems to public art programs.

The environmental graphic designer plans, designs and specifies sign systems and other forms of visual communication in the built and natural environment. Environmental graphic design serves three basic functions: to assist users in negotiating through space, by identifying, directing, and informing; to visually enhance the environment; and to protect the safety of the public.

Membership

Membership is available in the following categories: Professional, Associate, Allied, Industry, Student, Institutional and Artisan. For more information, contact the Membership Coordinator.

Activities

The SEGD national conference is held each year in the summer at a Design School. Recent themes have included wayfinding, design collaboration, and design education. The conference includes lectures, workshops, an awards ceremony, and the annual Trade Show.

SEGD also holds Regional Meetings each year in different areas of the country. SEGD local mixers are organized by SEGD members across the United States year round.

Awards

The SEGD awards recognize outstanding achievements and significant contributions made to the profession in environmental graphic design. These awards are presented annually at the national conference.

SEGD Annual Design Competition: open to members and non-members, deadline for entries in May.

SEGD Fellow Award: presented for outstanding individual contribution to the Society and the field.

Insight Award: given to an individual or organization for promoting understanding and awareness of environmental graphic design.

Angel Award: given to an individual for promoting awareness of the values of the profession and for contributing to the programming and direction of SEGD.

Student Grant Award: presented to students pursuing a career in the field, deadline for applications is November.

Publications

Messages: The society's quarterly publication provides members and subscribers with lively feature articles exploring topics of the field. Also includes resource listings, in-depth profiles of members, technical column, advertising and SEGD membership news.

The Professional Firm Directory: This directory, published in 1991, profiles SEGD professional member firms.

The Resource Directory: This literature includes an SEGD membership directory, bylaws, and a complete bibliography.

Technical publications and bulletins: *The System of Classification* is part of SEGD's work to improve and standardize sign descriptions; *Sourcebook One "Materials and Technologies,"* is a comprehensive description of the materials, techniques and technology currently in use in the field; *Sourcebook Two "Specifications Guide,"* provides general guidelines to aid designers in specifying environmental graphics.

Special Programs

The SEGD Education Foundation, the charitable arm of the SEGD, was created to address critical and timely educational issues of interest to the profession. SEGD has been awarded four grants from the National Endowment for the Arts. With these grants, SEGDEF developed a Model Curriculum for environmental graphic design; created a new national system of recreation symbols signs for use in over 7,000 Federal, State and local parks; developed reproductive artwork and user guidelines for a national standard of Industrial and Consumer Safety Symbols to help safeguard the health and safety of millions of workers and consumers; and developed Part I: The Visual Collection of a national archive for environmental graphic design. For the results of the grants, contact the SEGD.

Tracy Turner Design Inc.

Tracy Turner Design Inc.
30 West 22nd Street
New York / New York
10010

212.989.0221
212.989.0249 Fax

Other Clients Include

Disney Development
Company

Suntec City Development
Pte Ltd.

Regent International
Hotels

Olympia & York

Carnegie Hall Corporation

Crocker & Company

Morgans Hotel Group
 Morgans
 The Royalton
 Paramount

Citicorp

Canadian Imperial Bank
of Commerce

Memorial Sloan-Kettering
Cancer Center

Philip Morris Companies

IBM Corporation

Rockrose Development

New Otani

**Architectural Clients
Include**

**Pei, Cobb, Freed &
Partners**
New York City

**Kohn Pedersen Fox
Associates**
New York City

**James Stewart
Polshek & Partners**
New York City

**Cooper Carry
Associates Inc.**
Washington DC

**Arata Isozaki &
Associates**
Tokyo
New York City

**Tsao & McKown
Architects**
New York City
Singapore

**Kohn Pedersen Fox
Conway Associates Inc.**
New York City

**Kallman McKinnell
& Wood**
Boston

A full service design firm
specializing in corporate
and project identity,
printed graphics,
architectural signage and
graphics, hotel amenities,
and product design, from
preliminary design to
fabrication and
installation management.

Photo Credits

Stephen C. Traves
Graham Uden

■ N. H. Fedder Associates, Inc.

N.H. Fedder Associates Inc.
10 Tulip Avenue
Floral Park / New York
11001

516.775.6529
718.343.3344
516.354.1171 Fax

Full-service architectural lighting design firm including custom fixture design, optics, and dimming. More than 275 commercial and residential projects completed to date.

1

2

3

Projects Include

Yokohama Convention Center
Exterior lighting
Yokohama, Japan

Aquaduct Race Track
Jamaica, NY

Sky Chef's Restaurants:
  Newark Airport
  Palm Beach Airport

First Boston
5 World Trade Center
New York City

Air Vita
Phoenix Airport
Phoenix, AZ

NBC Third Floor News Room
New York City

Chambrel at Westlake
Westlake, OH

American Airlines
Admirals' Club:
  Kennedy Airport
  LaGuardia Airport
  (New York City)
  Logan Airport,
  (Boston, MA)

American Museum of
Natural History
(Phases I, II, & III)
New York City

Hyatt Key West
Key West, FL

Photo Credit

1. Scott Frances

2,3. George D. Miller

Selected Projects

1. Don Carter's Office
New York City
Interior Designer:
IFA
New York City

2, 3. Sky Chef's Restaurant
Ft Lauderdale Airport
Interior Designer:
The Office of Phil George
New York City

■ Specialized Services

**Boston Chapter of Industrial Designers Society of America
Information**

Alphabetical Listing

SP

IDSA Boston Chapter:

112 Beech Street
Roslindale, MA 02131

617.469.5416

Attention:
Elizabeth Goodrich
Chairman

IDSA is the national organization of professionals who design products, equipment, instruments, furniture, toys, transportation, packaging, exhibits, environments, and information systems. Founded in the 1930's, IDSA promotes the design profession, lobbies for design related issues, and provides services and programs to help industrial designers continue their professional development.

The Boston Chapter of IDSA holds periodic meetings focusing on design issues, presentations by design luminaries, new technologies, and related arts and cultural developments. We seek to provide an opportunity for design professionals to meet and exchange information in the interest of building the design community in Boston. We also distribute a newsletter which discusses our upcoming events for the season and sponsor seminars for professional development.

Membership in IDSA is broken into five categories: Member, Associate Member, and International Member, which require that the candidate have an undergraduate degree in design or ten years of experience in the field; Student Member; and Affiliate Member, which does not require a design background.

IDSA sponsors a National Conference and District Conferences each year. Held in the summer, the *IDSA National Conference* emphasizes design interaction with presentations by pacesetters on design, creativity, business, and cultural issues. The 1992 National Conference will be held in San Francisco. All IDSA members are eligible to enter the *Industrial Design Excellence Awards* which are held each spring. IDSA announces the winners at the National Design Conference and publicizes the winning entries to the design community along with business, trade, and general press.

IDSA National publishes the Directory of Industrial Designers; periodicals including the journal Innovation, the newsletter Design Perspectives, and annual studies on design management.

IDSA provides an *Ethics Advisory Council* which advises in matters regarding ethical conduct and moderates in ethical disputes. The *Code of Ethics* is published in the IDSA directory each year.

■ Valley Bronze of Oregon

Valley Bronze of Oregon
PO Box 669
307 West Alder Street
Joseph / Oregon
97846

503.432.7551
800.472.3970 Toll Free
503.432.0255 Fax

Artist Clients Include

Mick Brownlee

George Carlson

Chester Fields

Jan Fisher

Dorothy Fowler

Lorenzo Ghiglieri

Veryl Goodnight

Walt Matia

Jacques & Mary
Regat

Richard Stiers

Stan Wanlass

A full-service art foundry specializing in the production of monumental sculpture for architectural settings. Capable of undertaking point-up enlargements and model making. Casting in bronze, sterling silver, fine silver, stainless steel, and cast iron. On-site stone and wood base making, engineering, and installation services available.

Photo Credit

David Jensen

■ Dennis Earl Moore Productions, Inc.

137 Atlantic Avenue
Brooklyn Heights / New York
11201

718.875.8024
718.522.4358 Fax

Makes the use of film and electronic imaging available as raw building materials important to the architect and environmental designer. Focus of independent and collaborative work is twofold:

Video: The use of multi-image video as a 3-dimensional component that complements and articulates public spaces.

Film: Concept, design, and production of hybrid large scale film presentations that interpret, inspire, and entertain within defined spaces such as orientation areas, IMAX/OMNIMAX theaters, museums, and World's Fairs.

Worldwide project experience. Strength in concept development encourages participation from project inception.

Selected Projects

1. *Flyers*
First IMAX/OMNIMAX narrative film

2. *Video Lab*
60 Screen Video Assemblage research setting simulation

3, 5. *Videohenge* Panorama 120 Screen, 3-Dimensional Walkthru Video Environment

4. *Living Planet*
IMAX/OMNIMAX film (70mm - 75'x100' screens)

Reflections
1984 Louisiana World's Fair Unique Dual 35mm Over/Under Screen Format

RoboShoe
Six Axis Robotic Arm With Video Camera in Combination With 36 Monitor Stand-On-Floor Environment

Meet the Biospherians
Interactive Video Theater Incorporating Live Performance

Clients Include

SC Johnson Wax

1984 World's Fair
Petroleum Industries Pavilion

Nike, Inc.

Conoco, Inc./DuPont

Smithsonian Institution
National Air & Space Museum

Space Biospheres Ventures
Biosphere 2

■ Shenandoah Timberworks, Inc.

Shenandoah
Timberworks, Inc.
1005 South 5th Street
Hamilton / Montana
59875

406.363.6491

SP **101**

Custom timber framing, classic joinery, and innovative applications, including the bonding of timbers to metal frames for a more pleasing and satisfying appearance. Handcrafted workmanship for both residential and commercial design.

Architectural Clients Include

Hagman & Yaw Architects
Aspen, CO

Dynamic Design
Hamilton, MT

Stoskopf / Architects
Tulsa, OK

Photo Credit
William Meriwether

Other Clients Include

Hansen Construction, Inc.

Timberhouse Post & Beam

The Hilley Company

■ Karman Ltd.

Karman Ltd.
Architectural Products
7931 Deering Avenue
Canoga Park/California
91304

818.888.3818
818.888.3029 Fax

Selected Projects

Manufactures and installs high quality products fabricated from aluminum, brass, copper, stainless steel, glass, acrylic, and fiberglass.

Illuminated and non-illuminated products for interior and exterior placement: directories, pylons, letters, and neon, produced through processes that include art preparation, phototypesetting, silk screening, spray painting, gold leafing, etching, and sandblasting.

Specializes in complete signage projects for hotels, hospitals, schools, shopping malls, airports, parking structures, and libraries.

1

3

2

1, 2. Dolphin Hotel
Orlando, FL
Architect:
Michael Graves
New York City
Graphic Designer:
Arias Associates
Palo Alto, CA

3. Manulife Insurance Building
Los Angeles
Architect:
A.C. Martin & Associates
Los Angeles

4. Fossil Creek
Fort Worth, TX
Developer:
Woodbine Development Company
Dallas

UCSF Medical Center & Library
Graphic Designer:
Cummings Design
Santa Monica, CA

Chicago Hilton & Towers
Interior Designer:
Frank Mingus Design
Atlanta

South Coast Plaza
Newport Beach, CA
Architect:
Architect Pacifica Ltd.
Newport Beach, CA

Awards

IBD Gold 1980

IBD Silver 1983

PRINT Casebook Certificate of Excellence 1984

SEGD Bronze 1991

■ Ken Lieberman Laboratories, Inc.

Ken Lieberman
Laboratories, Inc.
118 West 22nd Street
New York / New York
10011

212.633.0500
212.675.8269 Fax

Other Clients Include

AT&T
American Express
Eastman Kodak Company
Grumman Corporation
National Audubon Society
Sports Illustrated
Magazine
Madison Square Garden
Kellogs Corporation
Kimberly Clark Corporation
Bristol Myers Squibb
Nikon Inc.
Olympus Corporation
Life Magazine
Merck & Company

**Architectural Clients
Include**

**Hellmuth, Obata &
Kassabaum**
St. Louis, MO

**Skidmore, Owings &
Merrill**
New York City

The Spector Group
North Hills, NY

Eisenman Architects
New York City

Olympia & York
New York City

Custom laboratory creating
photographic prints to any
size from art, renderings,
slides and negatives.
Offered as well are
complete framing and
mounting services, and an
extensive selection of
images suitable for wall
decor and display.

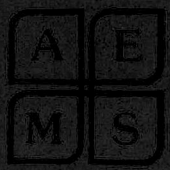

 **American Engineering Model Society**

National Office:

American Engineering Model Society
The Engineering Center
One Walnut Street
Boston, MA 02108

617 248 1928

Attention:
Ms. Paula Golden
Executive Director

Philosophy and Purpose

The American Engineering Model Society (AEMS) promotes and serves the interests of professional model-makers worldwide.

The objectives of the society are:

- To provide for the interchange of ideas among its members, to arrange for the collection and dissemination of information related to the use of physical models through publications, papers, seminars, and expositions.

- To educate the industrial public regarding the uses, applications, and advantages of physical models in industry, science, and government.

- To recognize those individuals engaged in the use of physical models and especially their outstanding accomplishments.

- To actively engage in a cooperative effort with other societies with mutual interests.

- To engage in a cooperative effort with the educational community to develop modeling as a vocation.

Membership

Membership in AEMS is open to individuals or organizations with an interest in the professional fabrication or use of physical models.

There are four grades of personal membership: Student, Individual, Emeritus and Honorary. There are two grades of organizational membership: Sustaining and Sponsoring.

To provide greater participatory opportunity among regional members the AEMS is endeavoring to establish a network of regional chapters. Currently chapters exist in Milwaukee/Wisconsin, Chicago.

Organizing efforts are underway in: Boston, San Francisco, Atlanta, Dallas, Seattle.

Awards

Outstanding Contribution Award
Awarded at the discretion of the Board of Directors in recognition of exemplary career service to the AEMS and outstanding contribution to its success.

President's Award
Awarded at the discretion of the Board of Directors in recognition of exemplary contributions in the use and promotion of scale models and to the success of the AEMS.

Highest Achievement Award
Awarded at the discretion of the Executive Committee for superlative contributions in the use and promotion of scale models.

Rasmussen Memorial Scholarship Award
"The Ronald A. Rasmussen Memorial Scholarship Award is to be given annually to a second year model making student best exemplifying the unselfish character and integrity of Ronald Rasmussen. Sponsored by the AEMS and funded by private donations from across the nation, the goal of this gift is to continue Ron Rasmussen's motivation, encouragement, and support of the model-makers of tomorrow."

Activities

National Convention
Indian Lakes Resort
Chicago, Illinois, May 15-16, 1992

Publications

AEMS Newsletter (6 issues/year)

Membership Directory (annual)

Catalogue of Services (annual)

Model making Bibliography (annual)

Seminar Papers (by event)

Special Programs

- Reference Library

- "Adventures in Scale Modeling" PBS-TV series

- Education Symposia at design schools & technical colleges nationwide

- Professional Development Workshops

- Rasmussen Memorial Scholarship Fund

- NICET Certification

- Member Model Photo Display at National Seminar.

Miscellaneous

Special Interest Groups

To address the growing diversity and complexity of professional model making skills, the AEMS has created Special Interest Groups (SIG's). Each SIG acts as a committee reporting to the National Board of Directors issues of interest and concern to that SIG. Currently SIG's represent the following areas:

Architecture
Forensic/Litigation
CADD/CAM
Piping
Display/Exhibit
Prototype
Engineering
Special Effects

■ Einer Model Company

Einer Model Company
412 113th Street
Arlington / Texas
76011

817.633.5644
817.633.3759 Fax

Architectural Clients Include

JPJ Architects
Dallas

Trammell Crow Company
Dallas
Austin
Charlotte, NC
Chicago

Dahl Braden PTM Inc.
Dallas

Harper Kemps Clutts & Parker
Dallas

Ray Bailey Architects
Houston

Harold E. Kaemmerling Architect
Lufkin, TX

RTKL
Dallas

Other Clients Include

Wyndham Hotel Company

Sea World of Texas

LARC
(Dallas)

Island Development
(Corpus Christi, TX)

Freeman Exhibit Company

Selected Project

Information Center
Seaworld of Texas
San Antonio, TX
Client:
Sea World of Texas
San Antonio, TX

■ Knoll Architectural Models, Inc.

Knoll Architectural Models
15752 Crabbs Branch Way
Rockville / Maryland
20855-2620

301.258.5212
301.670.9754 Fax

Professional model maker since 1965. Precisely scaled architectural models brought to life.

Affiliated with the American Institute of Architects, the SMPS, and the American Society of Landscape Architects.

Clients Include

Wisnewski, Blair & Associates, Ltd.

EDAW, Inc.

Skidmore, Owings & Merrill

Notter, Finegold & Alexander

Hartman-Cox Architects

Daniel, Mann, Johnson & Mendenhall

Keyes, Condon & Florence

Davis & Carter, PC

Leo A. Daly Company

Henningson, Durham & Richardson, Inc.

CHK Architects & Planners

Marriott Corporation

STV-HD Nottingham

Hugh Newell Jacobsen, FAIA

O'Brien & Gere Engineers, Inc.

Specialties Include

Architectural

Land Planning

Site Development

■ Scale Models Unlimited

111 Independence Drive
Menlo Park / California
94025

800.DIAL.SMU Toll Free
415.324.2111 Fax

320 West Ohio Street
Chicago / Illinois
60610

312.943.8160
312.943.9366 Fax

Selected Projects

1. 77 West Wacker Drive
Chicago
Developer:
The Prime Group
Chicago

2. 343 Sansome
San Francisco
Developer:
Hines Interests
San Francisco

3. 125 High Street
Boston
Developer:
Spaulding & Slye
Boston

4. **LaserCAMM** ™
Computer-driven laser
cutter manufactured by
Scale Models Unlimited
to reduce cost, shorten
construction time, and
create the highest level
of detail and accuracy
obtainable.

Architectural Clients Include

John Burgee Architects
New York City

EDAW
Atlanta

Gensler & Associates
San Francisco

Hellmuth, Obata & Kassabaum, Inc.
San Francisco

Johnson Fain & Pereira Associates
Los Angeles

Jung / Brannen Associates, Inc.
Boston

Caesar Pelli
New Haven, CT

Perkins & Will
Chicago

Skidmore, Owings & Merrill
San Francisco
Chicago

Robert A.M. Stern
New York City

Services

Foam Topographic Models

Architectural Study Models

Site Plan Models

Detailed Marketing Models

Photo Superimposition

Laser Cutting

LaserCAMM ™ Sales

■ Exhibitgroup

Stan Zalenski
8401 Ambassador Row
Dallas / Texas
75247-4697

214.630.1441
214.630.6490 Fax

Exquisitely precise
architectural models
crafted for many of
the world's leading
developers and
architects, incorporating
meticulous design and
an unsurpassed sense
of reality.

Creative hands and
minds prevail, whether
the project requires the
miniaturization of ten
thousand acres to
topographic precision or
expressing a subtle
architectural element.

State-of-the-art
techniques blended with
traditional artistry and
craftsmanship.

**Architectural Clients
Include**

**Skidmore, Owings &
Merrill**
New York City

Kohn Pederson Fox
New York City

**Kevin Roche, John
Dinkeloo Associates**
Hamden, CT

**Cesar Pelli &
Associates**
New Haven, CT

DeStefano / Goettsch
Chicago, IL

**Keyes Condon Florance
Architects**
Washington, DC

The Irvine Company
Irvine, CA

Selected Project

191 Peachtree Tower
Atlanta
Architect:
**John Burgee
Architects**
New York City

Photo Credit

© Aker Photography

■ Architectural Photographers

American Society of Magazine Photographers Information

Alphabetical Listing

AP

ASMP

■ American Society of Magazine Photographers

National Office:

419 Park Avenue #1407
New York, NY 10016

212.889.9144

Attention:
Richard Weisgrau
Executive Director

Philosophy and Purpose

The American Society of Magazine Photographers (ASMP) was established in 1944 to further the interests of photographers and their profession. It remains the world's foremost organization of professional photographers with over 5,000 members in 35 chapters and across the United States and internationally. These professionals specialize in every area from documentary and photojournalism to corporate/industrial and advertising in print, tape and related visual media.

ASMP coordinates legal and legislative activities and provides a national legal referral system. Through litigation and friend-of-the-court briefs, ASMP has helped shape critical court decisions, establishing precedents that benefit professional photographers in such areas as taxation, copyright, and work-for-hire. ASMP's "Good Offices" program assists individual members through its national office staff resources.

Throughout the 45 years since its founding, ASMP has been at the forefront of the profession. The Society's response to rapid change in the communications field has generated exceptional levels of support. We look forward to enhancing this record in the future.

For our membership, the Architectural field involves photographing manmade structures, usually for illustrative or record-keeping purposes. For example, an architect may need photographs at different stages of a building's progress to show to the client. Other needs run from advertising a particular project in the real estate industry to surveying for the government.

Generally, the client may include the work in portfolios, brochures, slide shows, and professional architectural competitions; this is called "record and exhibition use." But photographs may not be distributed or reproduced in any way without additional clearance from the photographer. Subsequent editorial publication, publicity use by suppliers, tenants, or building owners, and advertising use by manufacturers, are important sources of income to the photographer.

Activities

ASMP has been a pioneer in compiling and disseminating information on compensation, economic issues and ethics. Special programs and seminars facilitate ongoing communication between photographers and the business communities they serve. Such activities have resulted in greater understanding between photographers and their clients, as well as aiding photographers on issues involving new technology and negotiation.

Publications

ASMP serves as a clearinghouse of photographic information for the industry. The society provides a variety of services and products including informational publications such as *Professional Business Practices in Photography* and the *Stock Photography* handbook, the monthly ASMP *Bulletin*, a series of brochures directed to photographers and clients, White Papers on current industry issues, and comprehensive health and studio/equipment insurance programs.

Since projects involving professional photography often have budgets based on aesthetic as well as practical concepts, the commissioning client should expect to pay a fair fee for use of the photographs. The ASMP Assignment Photography Monograph includes for the first time guidelines to help clients understand appropriate working arrangements in architectural assignment photography.

Jeff Blanton

Jeff Blanton Photography
5515 South Orange Avenue
Orlando / Florida
32809

407.851.7279
407.857.4272 Fax

Publications

Audio/Video Interiors
Private Clubs Magazine
Better Homes & Gardens
Times Mirror, Inc.
Meredith Corporation
Planning Ideas

Award-win
of residen
contract ir
exteriors,
centers, th
suburban I
Using stroi
graphics, a
create a sp
space and

■ Warren Jagger

Warren Jagger
150 Chestnut Street
Providence / Rhode Island
02903

401.351.7366
401.421.7567 Fax

Selected Projects

1. Joseph Abboud
Boston
Designer:
**Bentley LaRosa
Salasky**
New York City
(As featured in
Architectural Record,
September 1991)

2. The Hudson Companies
Providence, RI
Architect:
Ekman, Arp & Snider
Warwick, RI

3. The Pavilions at
Buckland Hills
Hartford, CT
Architect:
**Cambridge Seven
Associates**
Cambridge, MA

1

■ Warren Jagger

Warren Jagger
150 Chestnut Street
Providence / Rhode Island
02903

401.351.7366
401.421.7567 Fax

**Architectural Clients
Include**

**The Architects
Collaborative**
Cambridge, MA

ADD Inc.
Cambridge, MA

Boston Properties
Boston
Washington, DC

CUH2A
Princeton, NJ

**Graham Gund
Architects**
Cambridge, MA

**Homart Development
Company**
Chicago

Herman Miller Inc.
Zeeland, MI

**Jung Brannen
Associates, Inc.**
Boston

**Skidmore, Owings &
Merrill**
New York City

**The Stubbins
Associates**
Cambridge, MA

Publications

Architecture

Architectural Digest

Architectural Record

Contract

Metropolitan Home

Interiors

Interior Design

Progressive
Architecture

Restaurant &
Hotel Design

VM & SD

2

3

■ Don Wheeler

Don Wheeler,
Photographer
Studio C
1933 South Boston Avenue
Tulsa / Oklahoma
74119

918.587.3808

Represented by
Suzanne Craig
918.749.9424

Selected Projects

1. Emergency Medical
Services Authority
Tulsa, OK
Architect:
Fritz / Baily Architects
Tulsa, OK

2. Warren Place
Metropolitan Life
Insurance Company
Tulsa, OK
Architect:
**Thompson Ventulett,
Stainback & Associates**
Atlanta

3. AMOCO Master
Earth Station
Tulsa, OK
Architect:
Murray Jones Murray
Tulsa, OK

1

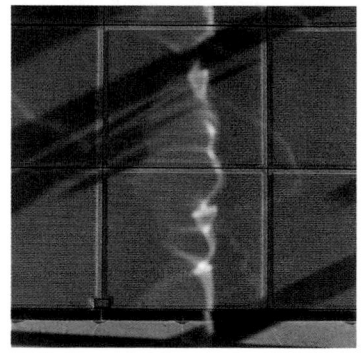

2

3

Architectural Clients Include

CDFM
Kansas City, MO

**Frankfurt Short &
Bruza Associates**
Oklahoma City

HTB, Inc.
Oklahoma City

MATRIX
Tulsa, OK

**Page Zebrowski
Architects**
Tulsa, OK

Over 20 years of providing
photography services to
architecture, interior
design, and development
firms in the Southwest.

Degree: BA in
Architectural Design,
Oklahoma State University

Member: American
Society of Magazine
Photographers.

■ Jennie Jones, Inc.

Jennie Jones, Inc.
One Cleveland Center
Suite 2900
1375 East Ninth Street
Cleveland / Ohio
44114

216.861.3850
216.861.4515 Fax

Specializing in architectural photography, including interiors, exteriors, models, construction progress photography, and full HABS/HAER documentation for the National Park Service.

Selected Project

Music & Communications Building
Cleveland State University
Cleveland, OH
Client:
Van Dijk, Johnson & Partners
Cleveland, OH

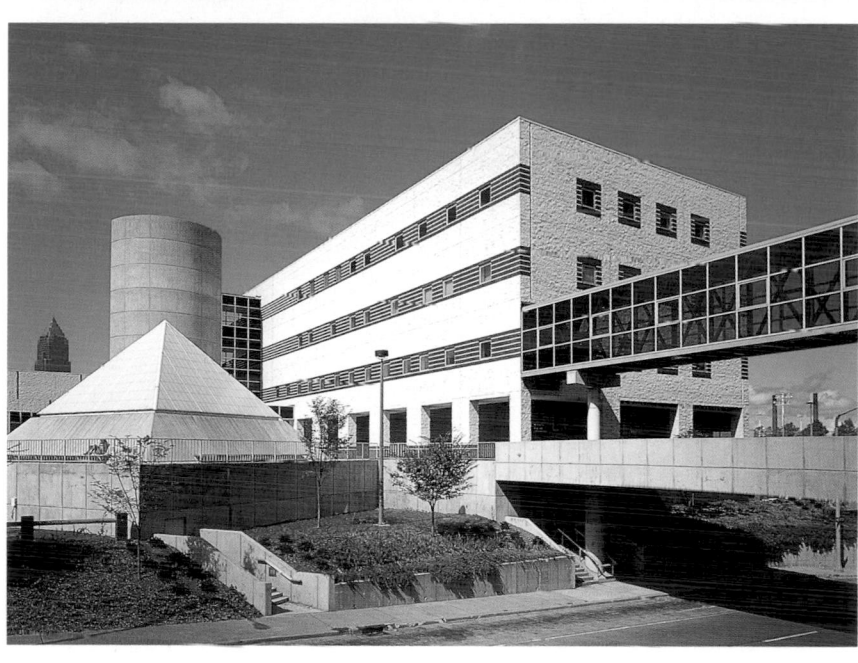

■ Sam Gray

Sam Gray Photography
23 Westwood Road
Wellesley /
Massachusetts
02181

617.237.2711

Portfolio available for a
personal presentation.

■ InSite

Glenn Cormier
828 K Street #305
San Diego / California
92101

619.237.5006
619.231.6624 Fax

Peter Malinowski
PO Box 20264
Santa Barbara / California

805.962.3870
805.962.6202 Fax

A complete list of magazine, architectural, and interior design clients is available on request.

Call or fax your request for an 8-page color brochure showing recent work.

Member: American Society of Magazine Photographers

Selected Projects

1,2. Hyatt Regency
at Aventine
La Jolla, CA
Architect:
Michael Graves
Princeton, NJ

3. Siegal Residence
Boca Raton, FL
Architect:
Barry Berkus
Santa Barbara, CA

4. Landsberg Residence
Temecula, CA
Architect:
Ken Kellog
San Diego, CA

1

3

2

4

■ Scott Miles

Landmark Photography
14 Mill Stream Road
Stamford / Connecticut
06903

203.968.2696

Architectural photography
skillfully produced to
communicate the talents
of the design team.

■ Richard Dale McClain

Richard Dale McClain
2212 South West Temple
Suite 6
Salt Lake City / Utah
84115

801.487.2112
800.728.9656 Toll Free

Committed to photographic artistry using careful lighting, attention to detail, and carefully chosen perspective to capture the essence of interiors and exteriors for architects, interior designers, and contractors.

**Architectural Clients
Include**

FFKR
Salt Lake City, UT

**Mediplex Medical
Building Corporation**
Dallas

Brixen & Christopher
Salt Lake City, UT

**Niels Valentiner
Associates**
Salt Lake City, UT

Martin / Martin
Salt Lake City, UT

**Pasker Gould Ames
Weaver**
Salt Lake City, UT

**Jacobsen
Construction**
Salt Lake City, UT

Member: American
Society of Magazine
Photographers

■ David Franzen

Franzen Photography
746 Ilaniwai Street
Suite 200
Honolulu / Hawaii
96813

808.537.9921
808.528.2250 Fax

Servicing the architectural, construction, and corporate markets for over 18 years.

Published extensively both nationally and internationally.

Architectural Clients Include

Kajima Associates
Los Angeles

Bechtel International
San Francisco

HKS Inc.
Dallas

Fletcher Pacific
Honolulu, HI

Ellerbe Becket
Santa Monica, CA

AIA Journal
Washington, DC

McConnell Dowell
Auckland, New Zealand

Wimberly, Allison, Tong & Goo
Honolulu, HI

Selected Project

Hawaii Prince Hotel
Honolulu, HI
Architect:
Ellerbe Becket
Santa Monica, CA

■ M. Lewis Kennedy, Jr.

M. Lewis Kennedy, Jr.
2700 Seventh Avenue South
Le Partenaire Creative
Facility
Birmingham / Alabama
35233

205.252.2700
205.252.2701 Fax

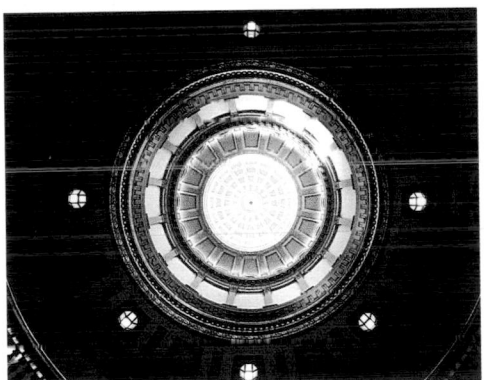

Distinctive images for architects, designers, builders, manufacturers, and publications.

Extensive location shooting cababilities. Modern studio with staff and in-house processing labs.

Portfolio and client list are available on request.

Member: American Society of Magazine Photographers; Society for Marketing Professional Services; and American Institute of Graphic Artists.

■ Colin McRae

Colin McRae
1061 Folsom Street
San Francisco / California
94103

415.863.0119
415.558.0485 Fax

Publications

Architectural Record

Architecture

Business Week

Communication Arts

Designers West

Home Magazine

House & Garden

Interior Design

Interiors

Metropolitan Home

Newsweek

Progressive
Architecture

Time

■ Colin McRae

Colin McRae
1061 Folsom Street
San Francisco / California
94103

415.863.0119
415.558.0485 Fax

Clients Include

Esherick Homsey
Dodge & Davis

Gensler & Associates

Hellmuth Obata &
Kassabaum

Holland East & Duvivier

Holt Hinshaw Pfau Jones

Kaplan McLaughlin & Diaz

STUDIOS Architecture

Whisler-Patri

Ahmanson Development
Company

Apple Computer

BankAmerica Corporation

Bramalea Pacific

Campeau Development
Company

Dupont

Eastman Kodak Company

Prudential

US Air

Wells Fargo Bank

■ Barbara White

Barbara White /
Architectural Photography
712 Emerald Bay
Laguna Beach / California
92651

714-494-2479
800.237.2479 Toll Free

826 East Florida Avenue
Suite G-6
Denver / Colorado
80231

Patience to arrange for the optimum lighting. Insight to frame from the perfect perspective. Clarity of vision to extract the essence of a setting.

Portfolio and client list available on request.

Publications

American Photographer
Architectural Record
Audio / Video Interiors
Business Interiors
Designer Specifier
Designers West
Interior Sources
Laguna
Orange Coast
Orange County
Professional Builder
Southern California
Home & Garden
South Coast
Sun Coast
Architect/Builder

Selected Project

Prime Ticket Network
Los Angeles
Interior Designer:
**Andrew Gerhard
Interiors, Ltd.**
Rancho La Costa, CA

■ Beth Singer

Beth Singer Photographer,
Inc.
25741 River Drive
Franklin / Michigan
48025

313.626.4860
313.932.3496 Fax

Clients Include

Des Rosiers Architects,
Inc.

General Motors
Corporation
(Argonaut AEC)

Ghafari Associates, Inc.

Giffels Associates, Inc.

Greiner, Inc.

Harley Ellington Pierce
Yee Associates, Inc.

Howard, Needles,
Tammen & Bergendoff

Albert Kahn Associates

Masco Corporation

Prudential Property Co.

Victor Saroki Associates

Sikes, Jennings & Kelley

Robert A. M. Stern

Sub-Zero Freezer Company

Publications

AIA Place

Architectural Record

Athletic Business

Better Homes & Gardens

Builder

Builders Design &
Construction

Business Facilities

Commercial Renovation

Contract Magazine

Designer Magazine

Detroit Monthly

Fine Homes

Kitchen & Bath Business

Professional Builder

The Quarton Group

Tokyo Business

Member: ASMP and SMPS

Affiliate Member: AIA,
Detroit Chapter

■ Paul E. Burd

Paul E. Burd Photography
300 East Hydraulic Street
Yorkville / Illinois
60560

708.553.7510

Publications

Chicago Magazine
Estate Magazine
Country Home Magazine
Popular Mechanics
Specifying Engineer

Commercial and editorial
photography with an
emphasis on dramatic
lighting and a strong
sense of design.

■ Campbell & Kamphaus

C & K Photographics
Philip Grussenmeyer
Stephen Pyle
Rural Route 8
Box 95
Union School Road
Decatur / Illinois
62522

800.777.8188 Toll Free
217.963.2135 Fax

Photography of interiors, exteriors, and models for architects, developers, and designers. Specializing in publication, advertising, and documentation.

Member. Professional Photographers of America ("Q" rating); American Society of Magazine Photographers; and the American Institute of Architects (Central Illinois Chapter)

Clients Include

BLDD Architects

LZT & Associates

Philip Swager & Associates

Henneman Raufiesen

Architectural Spectrum

Christner Partnership

Battielle Corporation

Caterpillar

Corn Products Company

Tate & Lyle

Bunn Corporation

Archer Daniels Midland

Construx of Illinois

Ultimate Interiors

Hilton Hotels
(Los Angeles)

Awards

Illinois Photographer of the Year 1991

Illinois Commercial Photographer of the Year 1989, 1991

Kodak International Gallery Award Recipient 1985, 1989, 1990, 1991

Epcot Gallery Exhibition 1985, 1989, 1990, 1991

■ Mel Curtis

Mel Curtis
2400 East Lynn Street
Seattle / Washington
98112

206.323.1230

Represented by
Donna Jorgensen
Annie Barrett, Associate
206.634.1880

Portfolio available upon request.

See A/DC 2 for additional work.

■ Mert Carpenter

Mert Carpenter
Photography
202 Granada Way
Los Gatos / California
95030

408.370.1663
408.370.1668 Fax

Graphic, dramatic, and creative photography for architects and the building industry for over 15 years.

Architectural Clients Include

Field Paoli Architects
San Francisco

Koll Construction
Pleasanton, CA

DES Architects
Redwood City, CA

San Jose Redevelopment Agency
San Jose, CA

Rick Guidice Architect
Los Gatos, CA

Ruth & Going Architects
San Jose, CA

Karen Butera Inc. Interiors
Palo Alto, CA

Provident Development
Austin, TX

The Grupe Company
Stockton, CA

Hathaway Construction
San Jose, CA

■ John Gillan

John Gillan
Photography, Inc.
12168 SW 131st Avenue
Miami / Florida
33186

305.251.4784
305.388.2255 Fax

Selected Projects

1. Physics Building
University of Miami
Miami
Architect:
**Spillis Candela &
Partners, Inc.**
Coral Gables, FL

2. Offices of Zuckerman
Staeder Taylor & Evans
Miami
Interior Designer:
**Joyce / Snoweiss
Design Group**
Coconut Grove, FL

3. Pier 66 Resort
Fort Lauderdale, FL
Interior Designer:
Dawn Starling
Miami

1

2

3

**Architectural Clients
Include**

**Sandy & Babcock
Architects Planners**
San Francisco
Miami

**The Richie
Organization**
Boston
Sarasota, FL

**Chen & Associates
Incorporated**
Miami

**The Smith, Korach,
Hayet, Haynie
Partnership**
Miami

**The Nichols
Partnership Inc.**
Coral Gables, FL

Camar Graniti, SPA
Rome, Italy

The Prudential
Coral Gables, FL

Member: American
Society of Magazine
Photographers; Board of
Directors for South Florida
Chapter

■ Dan Ham

Dan Ham Photography
1350 Manufacturing #212
Dallas / Texas 75207

214.742.8700
214.638.1905 Fax

317 Burch Street
Box 6421
Taos / New Mexico 87571

505.751.0602
505.751.0602 Fax

Bob Swanson

Swanson Images
532 Lisbon Street
San Francisco / California
94112

415.585.6567

"The Ariaga House –
Majesty in Ruins", from the
book *Home Sweet Jerome*
(Jerome Headlands Press,
in progress), about the
National Historic Landmark
town of Jerome, Arizona.

"A minor theme through
all the stories told me
were their definitions of
Jerome, epitaphs etched
into their memories, like
the names on the
tombstones just outside of
town surrounded by
wrought iron cages that
kept coyotes from digging
up the graves."

Diane Rappaport
Home Sweet Jerome

■ Bob Swanson

Swanson Images
532 Lisbon Street
San Francisco / California
94112

415.585.6567

Publications

Architectural Record

Interiors

Designers West

Visual Merchandising &
Store Design

Architectural Lighting

Engineering News Record

Sound & Video Contractor

Architectural Clients Include

Robinson Mills & Williams
San Francisco

Backen Arrigoni & Ross
San Francisco

Erlich Rominger
Mountain View, CA

George Famous / AT&T
San Leandro, CA

Gensler & Associates
San Francisco

Daniel Mann Johnson & Menderhall
San Francisco

Plant Construction Company
San Francisco

Rudolph & Sletten
Foster City, CA

Bedford Properties
San Francisco

Bold design statements created through attention to detail, structural composition and nearly four decades of photographic and building industry experience.

■ Marco P. Zecchin

Image Center
Photographic Design
1219 Willo Mar Drive
San Jose / California
95118

408.723.3649

Architectural and interior
design photography
conveying the
professional's vision.

Publications

Builders & Contractor

Home

Home Ideas

House Beautiful

Northern California Home
& Gardens

Northwest Kitchens & Bath

Palo Alto Times
Home Magazine

Panorama / Italy

Professional Builder

Sweet's

■ Shields-Marley

Shields-Marley
Photography
117 South Victory Street
Little Rock / Arkansas
72201-1827

501.372.6148
501.374.2111 Fax

Selected Projects

1. University of Arkansas
at Fayetteville
Old Main Renovation
Architect:
**Mott Mobley McGowan
& Griffin**
Fort Smith, AR

2. Leisure Arts, Inc.
Architect:
**Brooks Jackson
Architects**
Little Rock, AR

Awards

AIA Design Awards
1987, 1988, 1989,1991

ADDY Award
1990, 1991

United States Air Force
Design Awards
1990, 1991

Arkansas Times
Interior Design Awards
1988, 1989, 1990

IABC Excellence in
Communications
1986, 1987, 1988

PRSA Prism Awards
1986

Blending photographic
technique with visual
ingenuity to capture the
art of the designer, on
location or in the studio.
See A/DC 2 for additional
work or call for a portfolio.

■ Douglas Peebles

Douglas Peebles
445 Iliwahi Loop
Kailua / Hawaii
96734

808.254.1082
808.254.1267 Fax

Specializing in interior and
exterior architectural
photography with an eye
towards the architect's
use of lighting.

All formats 4x5 to 35mm.
Large selection of aerial
photographs of Hawaii
available.

Member: American
Society of Magazine
Photographers

■ Fine Artists and Artisans

Artisan Societies' Information

Alphabetical Listing

Public Art / Sculpture

Architectural Detail and Elements

Glass

FAA

■ Artisan Societies

Numerous organizations help to network artists, artisans and crafts people with the architectural community. The following provided Architectural Design Collaborators with resources to help in A/DC's outreach this year.

American Craft Council Library
40 West 53rd Street
New York/New York 10019
212.956.3535

Arts Midwest
528 Hennepin Avenue
Suite 310
Minneapolis/Minnesota 55403
612.341.0255

Brick Institute of America
11490 Commerce Park Drive
Reston/Virginia 22091
703.620.0010

American Ceramics Magazine
15 West 44th Street
New York/New York 10036
212.944.2180

Baulines Craft Guild
Schoenmaker Point
Sausalito/California 94965
415.331.8520

Boston Museum of Fine Arts
465 Huntington Avenue
Boston/Massachusetts 02115
617.267.9300

IFRAA
Interfaith Forum on Religion, Art and Architecture
1777 Church Street, N.W.
Washington/D.C. 20036
202.387.8333

■ Venice Neon Company

Venice Neon Company
Michael Cohen
Connie Wexler Cohen
1221 Abbot Kinney Blvd.
Venice / California
90291

310.392.4041
310.314.4810 Fax

Specializing in innovative, site-specific design and project management for large-scale neon and mixed-media installations, at both private and public locations.

Member: Design Lighting Forum

Clients Include

Minnesota NBA Association

Arical Properties

Arthur Andersen & Company

Adams Publishing, Inc.

International Interiors, Inc.

Radisson Hotel

Clarion Hotel

Avnery Development

Photo Credits

Shin Koyama

Connie Cohen

Publications

Architectural Record Lighting

Lighting Dimensions

Signs of the Times

■ Rob Fisher

Environmental Sculpture
228 N Allegheny Street
Bellefonte / Pennsylvania
16823

814.355.1458
814.231.1344 Fax

Clients Include

Ball-Unimark Corporation
Carnegie Science Center
Carolina Corporate Center
City of Hamamatsu
(Japan)
DeBartolo Corporation
Gateway Science Center
(Philadelphia)
Howard Johnson Corp.
Kingdom of Saudi Arabia
Mellon Bank
New York Hilton
Osaka Hilton International
(Japan)
Playboy Corporation
Trump Corporation
Water Pollution Control
Federation
Westcor Partners (Arizona)

International lecturer on art and technology.

Bachelor of Science in Humanities, Engineering, and Visual Design, Massachusetts Institute of Technology (1961)

Fulbright Fellowship, University of Oslo (1962), University of Rome (1963)

Master of Industrial Design, Syracuse University (1965)

Other awards include Rockefeller Foundation Grant (1981); Meritorious Design, Vietnam Veterans Memorial (1981); Special Projects, Pennsylvania Council on the Arts (1986, 1987, and 1989).

Featured on CNN Science & Technology News and USIA Worldnet television; in Sculpture Magazine and Leonardo Journal; and in both national and international exhibitions.

Co-author of *The Design Continuum* (Van Nostrand Reinhold, NY, 1966).

Photo Credit
Al Payne

Selected Project

Symphony of the Air
Scottsdale, AZ 1991

■ Maryrose Carroll

Maryrose Carroll
1682 North Ada
Chicago / Illinois
60622

312.342.7282
312.248.8392 Fax

Clients Include

Sol LeWitt (artist)

Northwestern University

Inglis Art

Walter Netsch, AIA

Dayton Art Museum

Illinois State Art Museum

Selected Projects

1. *Bosk of Spring Trees*
Evanston, IL
Developer:
Rescorp, Inc.
Chicago

2. *In Dreams Begin Responsibilities*
Chicago, IL
Developer:
Metropolitan Structures
Chicago

3. *Three Trees*
San Diego
Developer:
Daley Corporation
San Diego, CA

4. *Lincoln Tree*
Springfield, IL
Client:
State Journal Register
Springfield, IL

Specializing in site-specific sculptural installations that combine organic and geometric elements. Permanent installations include freestanding outdoor and indoor sculpture in lightweight aluminum.

Katherine Holzknecht

Katherine Holzknecht
22828 57th Avenue SE
Woodinville / Washington
98072

206.481.7788

Creates unique mixed-media artworks for architectural spaces. Site-specific art results from collaboration with design professionals to produce innovative artworks that are well suited for the location.

Projects incorporate a variety of materials from high-tech and construction sources.

Specializing in full-spectrum colors and visual textures to enhance existing design features.

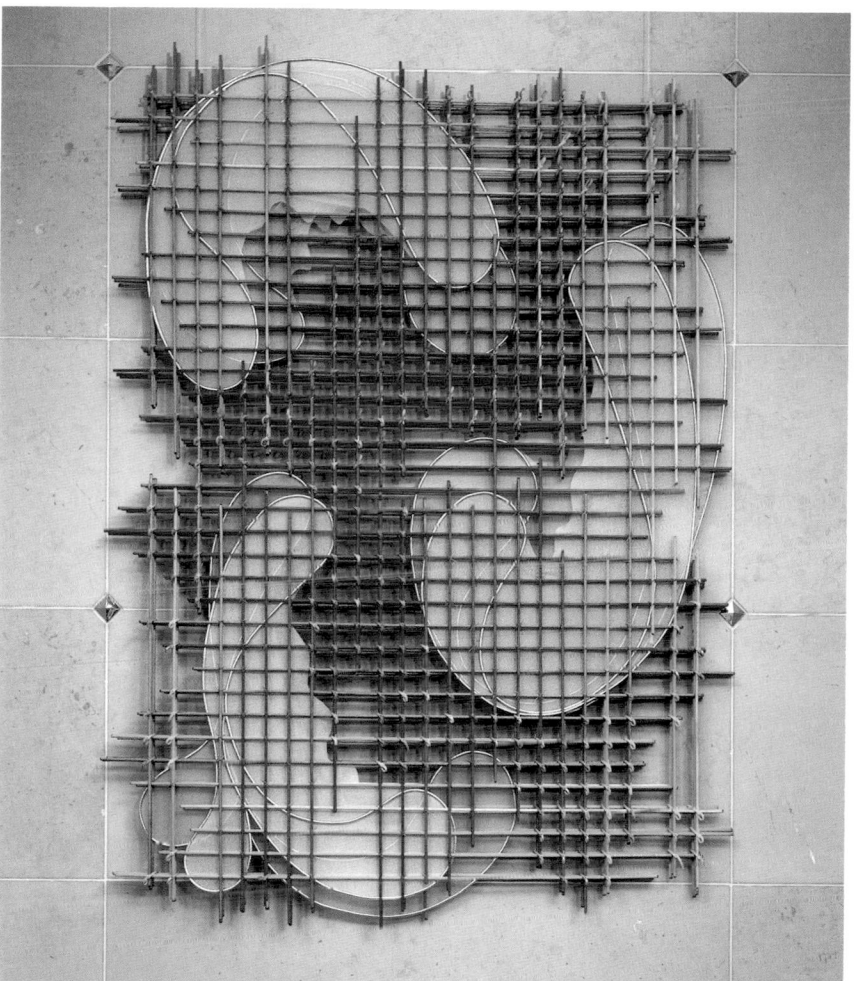

1

Selected Projects

1. Westlake Center Office Tower
Seattle
Developers:
Westlake Center Associates
Seattle
The Rouse Company
Seattle
Koehler McFayden & Company
Seattle

2. Shriners Hospital
Spokane, WA
Architects:
The NBBJ Group
Seattle
ALSC Architects
Spokane, WA
Art Agent:
Corporate Art West
Bellevue, WA

International Corporate Center at Rye, NY
Architect:
Papp Architects, PC
White Plains, NY
Developer:
The Gateside Corporation
Rye, NY

2

Photo Credit

1 Roger
   Schreiber
2. Alan Bisson

■ Karl Rosenberg

136 North 8th Street
Brooklyn / New York
11211

718.388.8168
212.475.2515

RD #1, Box 180
Andes / New York
13731

914.586.3067

Selected Projects

AT&T Eastern
Headquarters
galleria, atrium, and
executive office pieces
Architect:
Kohn Pederson & Fox
New York City

116 Inverness
exterior, lobby, and
atrium pieces
Architect:
C. Fentress
Denver, CO

Chesapeake & Potomac
Telephone
two atrium aerials
Architect:
D. Coupard
Rockville, MD

Linclay Center III
four-story waterfall piece
Architect:
HIXON
Cincinnati, OH

Other Projects Include

Raddison Hotels
(O'Hare, Downers Grove,
and Glenview)
three atrium aerials
Walden Investment
Company
Architect:
**Skidmore, Owings &
Merrill**
Chicago

Walden Galleria,
Berkshire Galleria, and
Poughkeepsie Galleria
Malls
five atrium aerials
Pyramid Companies of
Syracuse
Architect:
DAL PAS
Syracuse, NY

Sculptor producing multi-
media, site-specific art.

See A/DC 1 and 2 for
additional projects.

■ Brian Stotesbery

Brian Stotesbery
500 Molino Street
Suite 218
Los Angeles / California
90013

213.617.7987

Selected Projects

Image Cube
Computer-controlled
light sculpture
IDS Center
Minneapolis, MN
Client:
Olympus Corporation
Minneapolis, MN

Ascending Cross Section
Computer-controlled
light sculpture
Private Residence
Minneapolis, MN

Neon Gears
Electronic sculpture
Client:
Marquette National Bank
Minneapolis, MN

Laser Light Sculpture
IDS Center
Minneapolis, MN
Space planner:
Jamieson & Associates, Inc.
Minneapolis, MN

Lighting for Elevator
Private Residence
Wayzata, MN

Exhibitions

Museum of Neon Art
Los Angeles 1992

Centennial Alumni Exhibition
College of Art & Design
Minneapolis, MN 1986

Sci-Expo
San Diego, CA 1986

An Exhibition of
Light & Logic
Coffman Gallery
Minneapolis, MN 1984

Minnesota Museum of Art
St. Paul, MN 1977

Helen Euphrate Gallery
Cupertino, CA 1977

Pavilion for the Arts
Chicago 1977

Electric Art in Boxes
The Electric Gallery
Toronto, Canada 1976

Site-specific computer
and electronically
controlled artworks for
incorporation into public
spaces, including subway
stations, theater interiors,
building exteriors, and
outdoor sculptures. Video
featuring works in motion
is available upon request.

Franz Mayer Mosaics

Franz Mayer of Munich, Inc.
Artistic Mosaics
Stained Glass
343 Passaic Avenue
Fairfield / New Jersey
07004

201.575.4777
201.575.5588 Fax

Established in 1845. One of the leading international studios for artistic mosaics and stained glass.

All work completed in close collaboration with the independent artist / designer.

Offering full design, execution, and installation services.

Stained glass and mosaics created for thousands of public and ecclesiastical buildings around the world, many of which have been awarded landmark status.

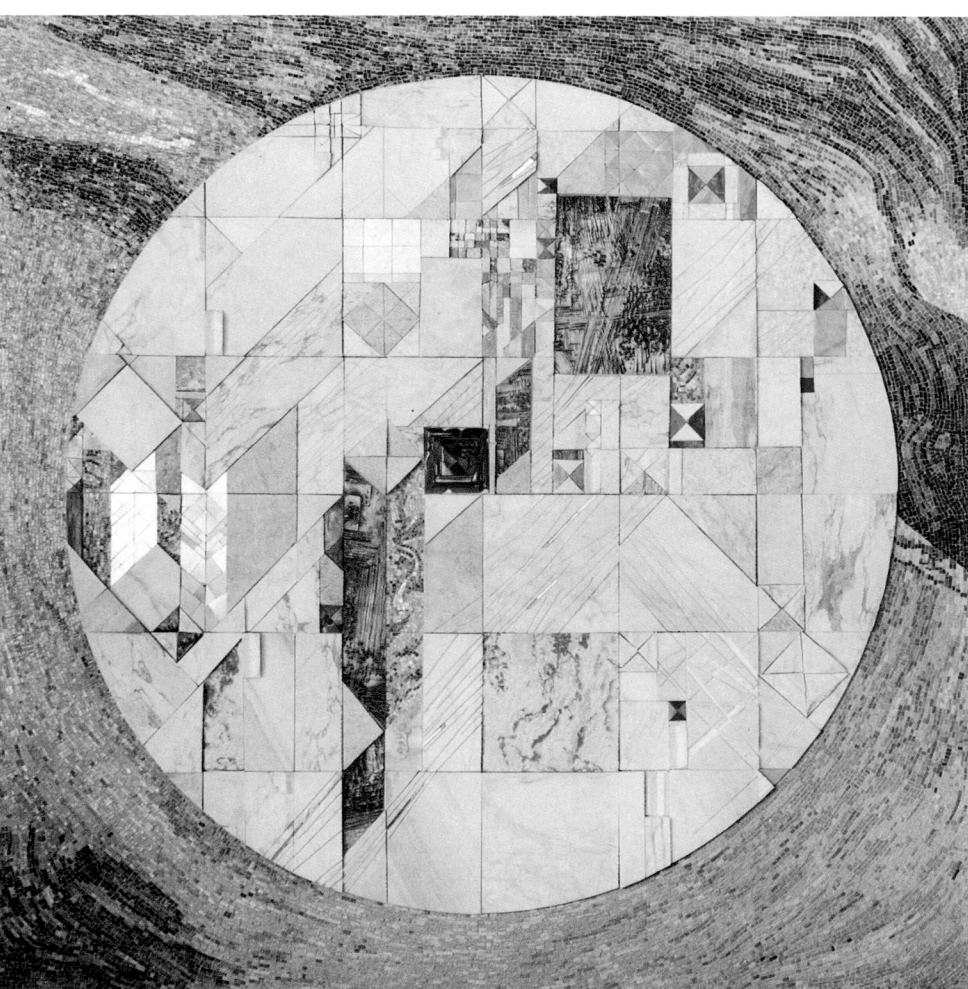

Selected Projects

Heart Tent
Artistic Glazing of Steel
Net Tent Construction
Diplomatic Club
Riyadh, Saudi Arabia
Artist / Architect:
Atelier Frei Otto

Freestyle
Ceramic Mural
Equitable Center
New York City
Artist:
Valerie Jaudon

Mosaic Triptych
1275 Pennsylvania Avenue
Washington, DC
Artist:
Miles Stafford Rolph

The Tongue of the Cherokee
Glass Ceiling
Carnegie Museum of Art
Pittsburgh, PA
Artist:
Lothar Baumgarten

Roman 'Tethys' Mosaic
Harvard Business School
Morgan Hall
Boston
Restoration of Mosaic Floor
(probably largest ancient mosaic in US)

■ M.C. CAROLYN

M.C. CAROLYN Sculptor &
Associates, Ltd.
316 Elm Avenue
Takoma Park / Maryland
20912

301.270.8094

Exhibitions

University of Maryland
University College
College Park, MD 1990

Art in Public Places
Rockville, MD 1991

Chautauqua Art Assoc.
Chautauqua Institute
Chautauqua, NY 1991

The Hodson Gallery
Frederick, MD 1990-91

Hakone Open Air Museum
Tokyo, Japan 1988

John F. Kennedy Center
Washington, DC 1988

Wallace Wentworth
Gallery (solo exhibition)
Washington, DC 1985, 1986

Capital Children's Museum
Washington, DC 1987

Allied Artists of America
National Arts Club
New York City 1986

Clients Include

University of Maryland
University College

National Museum of
Women in the Arts

Economic Development
Corporation

National Institute of
Health

Maryland-National Capitol
Park and Planning
Commission

The Thornton Collection
(Georgetown, KY)

Benedikt Wasmuth
(Munich, Germany)

St. Columba Catholic
Church
(Oxon Hill, MD)

Leonard A. Shapiro

David Evans

Unique benches, fountains,
and sculptures crafted
from stone and bronze by
an artist able to address
the technical requirements
of each site.

■ Archwood, Inc.

Archwood, Inc.
2109 Great Trails Drive
Wooster / Ohio
44691

216.264.4563
800.545.1312 Toll Free
(in Ohio & surrounding
states)
216.264.3935 Fax

Creating and restoring
fine furniture and
architectural pieces for
public and private spaces.

Works primarily with
architects and designers
on projects for businesses,
private homes, churches,
temples and colleges.

Maintains close working
relationships with stained
glass artists, sculptors,
metal fabricators, textile
artisans and other
craftspersons.

Established in 1981.

Selected Projects

1. Lectern (white oak)
First Presbyterian Church
Wooster, Ohio

2. Mirror
Neoclassical style
(mahogany)
Private Residence

3. Detail from dining table
Eastlake Victorian style
(walnut)
Private Residence

4. Restoration of 1901
Knabe grand piano
(rosewood)
Private Residence

Photo Credit
Tony Festa
Photography

Specialties Include

Fine Furniture

Architectural Woodwork

Conservation &
Restoration

John Luttmann

Luttmann Brothers
Woodcarving & Sign
Company
15 South Main Street
Phoenixville / Pennsylvania
19460

215.935.0920
215.933.9205 Fax

Signage, architectural ornamentation, and point of purchase displays.

Design through fabrication of contemporary, traditional, and historical signage. Ornamentation with an emphasis on relief and sculptural carving.

Large-scale dimensional pieces that integrate signage and sculpture, fabricated from Sign-Foam (a rigid polyurethane foam, available in sheet and block stock).

In-house mold making capability and casting facilities to meet quantity requirements.

Selected Projects

ARCO Chemical Company
Headquarters
Newtown Square, PA

Stoneridge Corporate
Center
Exton, PA

The Vanguard Group
Valley Forge, PA

Zoo Atlanta
Atlanta, GA

Hotel Cheyanne
Euro Disneyland
France

Mikasa...Lifestyles
Secaucus, NJ

Tiger Stop
National Zoological Park
Washington, DC

■ Modeworks Conservation

54 Leonard Street
New York / New York
10013

212.226.4079
212.226.9258 Fax

Columbus / Ohio
614.297.6844

Dallas / Texas
214.426.1334

Experts on historic
preservation and
conservation of major
monuments, mural
paintings and objects of
fine art, executed for
public agencies, museums
and private clients.
Consultation for historic
preservation, and
execution of decorative
painting.

1

Clients Include

1. Superintendent of Fine Art
Salerno, Italy

2. Justin Management
New York City

Department of Parks &
Recreation
New York City

Superintendent of Fine Art
Florence, Italy

The Wolfsonian
Foundation

Sotheby, Inc.

Safani Gallery

Monastery Certosa Di
Padula National Museum
Italy

Superintendent of Fine Art
Berlin, Germany

The Plaster Museum
Pietrasanta, Italy

2

■ Conrad Schmitt Studios

Conrad Schmitt Studios
2405 South 162nd Street
New Berlin / Wisconsin
53151

414.786.3030
800.969.3033 Toll Free
414.786.9036 Fax

Established in 1889.
Experienced in the
conservation of the
traditional, as well as
the creation of the
contemporary. Involved in
the preservation and
renovation of numerous
structures of architectural
and historic significance
across the country.
Whether working directly
with the client or through
the architect or designer,
the studio is an effective
part of the team,
achieving excellence
through the quality of
its art.

1

Selected Projects

1. Wang Center for the
Performing Arts
Boston
Architect:
**Notter Finegold &
Alexander**
Boston

Federal Building,
U.S. Courthouse
Milwaukee, WI
Client:
**General Services
Administration**
Chicago

University of Notre Dame
Sacred Heart Church
South Bend, IN
Architect:
Ellerbe Becket Company
Minneapolis, MN

Union Station
St. Louis, MO
Architect:
**Hellmuth, Obata &
Kassabaum**
St. Louis, MO

Waldorf-Astoria Hotel
New York City
Architect:
**Kenneth E. Hurd &
Associates**
Boston

Photo Credit
Copyright 1990
Roger Farrington

■ Glass

■ Pacific Art Glass

Pacific Art Glass
1200 College Walk
Suite 107
Honolulu / Hawaii
96817

808.537.3758
808.526.0736 Fax

Architectural Clients Include

Media Five
Honolulu
Australia

Gulstrom • Kosko Group
Honolulu

Leo A. Daly
Honolulu

Concept Design Group
Honolulu
Singapore

Lacayo Architects
Honolulu

AM Partners
Honolulu

Wimberly, Allison, Tong & Goo, Inc.
Honolulu

Other Clients Include

Hilton Corporation

Stark Ventures Ltd.

Mauna Lani Bay Resort

Toyota Motor Corporation

Bank of Hawaii

Royal Hawaiian Hotel

State of Hawaii

EEC Industries
(Canada)

Guam Hyatt Hotel

Matura Beach Resort
(Malaysia)

Mauna Kea Hotel

Obayashi Group

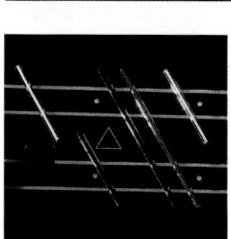

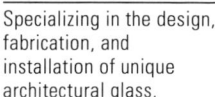
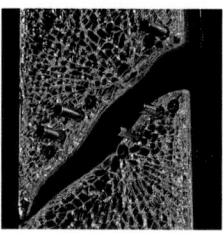

Specializing in the design, fabrication, and installation of unique architectural glass.

Photo Credits
Ed Espero
David Franzen

■ Frank Close

Frank Close
397 West Twelfth Street
New York / New York
10014

212.989.7039
212.807.8950 Fax

In collaboration with the architect, designer, and client, distinctive architectural glassworks are created using the unique color and refracting properties of blown, cut, bevelled, and etched glass.

Site-specific installations respond to surroundings, informed by quality of light, use of space, psychological environment, and architectural style.

Architectural Clients Include

Shepley Bulfinch Richardson & Abbott
Boston

RTKL Associates, Inc.
Baltimore

Tony Chi & Associates
New York City

Walz Design
New York City

Grad Associates
Newark, NJ

Guyon / Walton Inc.
Lexington, KY

Tom Lee Ltd.
New York City

Other Clients Include

IBM

Prudential Insurance Company

Phillips Academy (Andover,. MA)

Costain Group

Doral Country Club

Liberty National Bank

Pace University

Photo Credit
Walt Roycraft

■ J. Gorsuch Collins

J. Gorsuch Collins
8283 West Iliff Lane
Lakewood / Colorado
80227

303.985.8081
303.980.0692 Fax

Selected Projects

Zenith Restaurant
Denver, CO
Architect:
Gensler Architects
Denver, CO

Colorado Legislative
Services Building
Denver, CO
1% for the Arts Project

Littleton Hospital Chapel
Littleton, CO
Architect:
Davis Partnership
Denver, CO

Kaiser Permanente
Denver, CO
Architect:
Klipp Partnership
Denver, CO

St. Anne's Episcopal School
Denver, CO
Architect:
**Murato Outland
Architects**
Denver, CO

Specializing in works that exude originality and compatibility with the architectural setting, designed in collaboration with the architect.

Works incorporate a wide variety of techniques, often in combination with other materials or with other artists, providing interesting departures from previous works.

Custom blown, etched, fused, and beveled glass allow maximum versatility in texture. Smaller architectural accessories that complement the main installation are also available.

Delivery and installation possible both nationally and internationally.

Photo Credits
Hedrich Blessing
Kosloff Photography

■ Joel Berman

Joel Berman Glass
Studios, Ltd.
1-1244 Cartwright Street
Granville Island
Vancouver /
British Columbia
Canada V6H 3R8

604.684.8332
604.684.8373 Fax

Clients Include

Canadian Airlines
International

Canadian National
Railways

Towers Perrin

Four Seasons Hotel
(Vancouver)

Cathedral Place

Ferguson Gifford

Marine Building
(Vancouver)

Russell Du Moulin

Thompson Dorfman
Sweatman

Canadian Imperial Bank of
Commerce

Selected Projects

1. *Suspension*
Cable-hung, colored,
curved, and laminated
glass collage featuring
antique glass with
dichroic glass appliqué
Domestic Empress Lounge
Lester B. Pearson
International Airport
Toronto
Interior Design:
City Interiors Ltd.
Vancouver, BC (Canada)
and **BBA Design
Consultants**
Vancouver, BC (Canada)

2. Autonomous Collage
Colored, laminated glass
Towers Perrin
Vancouver, BC (Canada)
Interior Designer:
**Group 5 Design
Associates**
Vancouver, BC (Canada)

Specializing in the design
and fabrication of
successful architectural
glass art for commercial
interior space, with
emphasis on corporate
offices and building lobbies.
Work includes most forms
of flat, bent, and etched
glass as well as indoor and
outdoor glass sculpture.

■ Wilmark Studios

Wilmark Studios Inc.
177 South Main Street
Pearl River / New York
10965

914.735.7443

Clients Include

Albinas Elskus

Willy Malarcher

Ellen Mandlebaum

Yaraslava Mills

Brigitte Pasternak

Robert Pinart

Hendrik Vandeburgt

Efram Weitzman

Paul Wood

Photo Credit
Mark Liebowitz

Selected Projects

The National Arts Club
New York City
two skylight windows
Designer:
Albinas Elskus
New York City

St. Vincent Hospital Chapel
New York City
restoration & new stained
glass windows
Designer:
Hendrik Vandeburgt
Westwood, NJ

St. Luke's Church
Long Beach, CA
stained glass transoms
Designer:
Robert Pinart
Nyack, NJ

Sacred Heart Church
Cambria Heights, NY
ten stained glass windows
Designer:
Willy Malarcher
Englewood, NJ

National Cathedral
Washington, DC
four chapel windows
Designer:
Robert Pinart
Nyack, NY

Fabrication and
installation of leaded and
stained glass windows
employing various surface
treatments in a
collaborative process with
artist, architect, designer,
and clients.

■ Rohlf's Studio, Inc.

Peter A. Rohlf
Peter H. Rohlf
783 South Third Avenue
Mt. Vernon / New York
10550

914.699.4848
212.823.4545
212.823.4717 Fax

Collaborating on an international level to achieve the highest degree of integrity between art and architecture.

Creating and working in all mediums of leaded, stained, faceted, laminated, beveled, etched, and dimensional glass for liturgical and commercial commissions

Architectural Clients Include

Hardy Holzman Pfieffer
New York City

Beyer, Blinder, Belle
New York City

Yendo Associates
New York
Tokyo

Peter L. Gluck & Partners
New York City

James Stewart Polshek & Partners
New York City

Shope Reno Warton Associates
Greenwich, CT

**Kevin Roche
John Dinkeloo & Associates, Inc.**
Hamden, CT

Photo Credit
Steve Ostrow

Selected Project

Ferncliff Mausoleum
Hartsdale, NY
Architect:
Joseph J. Mangan, AIA
Hohokus, NJ

■ David Wilson

David Wilson Design
RD2 Box 121A
South New Berlin /
New York
13843

607.334.3015
607.334.7065 Fax

Designs, fabricates and
installs projects that
integrate art with
architecture.

Selected Projects

Corporate Boardroom,
Corning, Inc.
New York City
Architect:
**Kevin Roche John
Dinkeloo and Associates**
Hamden, CT

Ives Public Library
New Haven, CT
Architect:
**Hardy, Holzman, Pfeiffer
Associates**
New York City

St. Paul's Catholic Church
Tampa, FL
Architect:
The Ashford Group
Clearwater, FL

Photo Credit
Richard Walker

 Index

Alphabetical / State / Discipline Index

State / Discipline / Alphabetical Index